MODI'S BLUEPRINT FOR INDIA

Policy, Governance and Emerging Challenges

MODI'S BLUEPRINT FOR INDIA

Policy, Governance and Emerging Challenges

Editor

Anil Bhat

PENTAGON PRESS

Modi's Blueprint for India: Policy, Governance & Emerging Challenges
Anil Bhat (Editor)

First Published in 2014

ISBN 978-81-8274-788-3

Published by
PENTAGON PRESS
206, Peacock Lane, Shahpur Jat
New Delhi-110049
Phones: 011-64706243, 26491568
Telefax: 011-26490600
email: rajan@pentagonpress.in
website: www.pentagonpress.in

Branch:
Prime Arcade
Office #11
1154 Saifee Street
Opp. M.G.Road, Camp
Pune-411001
Email: pentagonpresspune@gmail.com

Printed at Aegean Offset Printers, Greater Noida, U.P.

CONTENTS

	Editor's Note	7
	Contributors	15
1.	The Beginning of the Modi Era *Siva Sivapragasam*	17
2.	For a Meaningful Engagement with Parliament *P D T Achary*	23
3.	Challenges for Narendra Modi on National Security and Related Foreign Policy *Anil Bhat*	31
4.	A Proposed National Security Agenda for Narendra Modi *Maj Gen GD Bakshi*	69
5.	India's Energy Security: Emerging Challenges *Talmiz Ahmad*	79
6.	Challenges of Indian Foreign Policy: Post-2014 Scenario *Sudhir Singh*	93
7.	What Should be Modi's Foreign Policy? *Pankaj Jha*	105
8.	Rapid Urbanisation Posing Huge Infrastructure Challenges *Sudipt Arora*	115
9.	Too Much on the Political, Diplomatic Plate for the BJP *Tripti Nath*	127

10. Challenges in the Educational System for Narendra Modi 135
Sheetal Jain

11. Good overnance in India: The Imperatives of Human Rights-Based Development Approach 151
Suresh R

12. Concerns for Women: The Vision for 21st Century 165
Ruchi Ramesh

13. Requirements for Road Safety in India 175
Piyush Tewari

Index 185

EDITOR'S NOTE

The world's largest democracy saw over 563 million votes being cast over a period of five weeks, resulting in a massive victory for the Bharatiya Janata Party (BJP) led by former thrice elected Chief Minister of Gujarat, Narendra Modi, who succeeded in reaching out to all parts of this vast nation during his campaign. While there is no doubt about Mr. Modi being the decisive factor for BJP's victory, this election's result is also a testimony to the high level of dissatisfaction and frustration of the Indian public with the scam-ridden Congress led United Progressive Alliance (UPA).

If India's 2014 election saga has been different from earlier ones or unprecedented, its genesis to a large extent, is the campaign launched by Anna Hazare. On April 5, 2011, Hazare began a fast unto death at Jantar Mantar in Delhi for a stronger anti-corruption Lokpal (Ombudsman) Bill in Parliament, which shook both India's public and its polity like never before. The public got shaken out of a stupor accumulated for over six decades on a diet of a dicey concoction of dynastic rule, vote-bank politics exploiting religion and caste, unbridled corruption, sycophancy, suppression/twisting of certain facts also amounting to altering history and disturbingly, repeatedly compromising disastrously on national security. The only exception on national security and foreign policy related to it was late Mrs. Indira Gandhi , who in 1967 and 1971 at least, showed her acumen and assertiveness in dealing with two hostile neighbours, as elaborated upon in my chapter of this book.

The sheer shrillness of the 2014 election campaign towards the end of the Congress dominated UPA 's two tenures should not come as a surprise at all. Chockablock with scams, mis-governance to absolute lack of governance, the wide range of multi-faceted corruption and almost six decades long run of taking the country for a ride in so many ways, Anna Hazare's initial phase of the movement of fasting from Jantar Mantar and the public response it received, sent shock waves all around Lutyen's New Delhi. Subsequent phases of this agitation fetched even wider and more intense response. Reactions of a section of India's Parliamentarians ranting about the supremacy and sanctity of the Parliament, which they had worked hard at compromising, only proved how stinging the blow of Hazare's expose was.

The Aam Admi Party's (AAP) massive victory, also very largely attributable to Hazare's campaign, came as the next telling blow to the Congress. But the developments that ensued leading to AAP's Arvind Kejriwal resigning as Delhi's Chief Minister only add grist to the mill that he/AAP may have been purchased by the Congress to counter BJP Narendra Modi. After getting drubbed by the BJP in Rajasthan, Madhya Pradesh and Chhattisgarh also, Congress, hit in its solar plexus and defeat in the 2014 general elections written large on the wall, is reported to have resorted to attempts to counter or limit the swelling wave of Narendra Modi by propping up/purchasing AAP.

Narendra Modi's country-wide campaign of well attended rallies has been marked by his airing many facts of India's history, assiduously suppressed by the Congress since Independence and some relevant ones since before Independence, as well as many lies or false claims of public welfare-related projects and other achievements made by the party. While the report card of the Congress party's performance in governance covering administration, foreign policy/diplomacy and worst of all national security has been poor, it has certainly not helped the Congress that out of the blue an Australian journalist Neville Maxwell suddenly wakes up and leaks out a part of the report on following India's humiliating defeat in the 1962 Sino-Indian war prepared by Lt. Gen. Henderson-Brooks and Brig. (later Lt. Gen.) Prem Bhagat.

As the war of words and barbs between the Congress and BJP's got harder and hotter, the BJP came out with a 58-page "chargesheet" on UPA's 10-year rule, condemning it as a "failure on all fronts" and accusing Sonia Gandhi and her son Rahul Gandhi, the Congress party's primeminesterial candidate of being equally guilty of all ills by exercising authority without responsibility. BJP launched an all-out attack on UPA government accusing it for its economic policies that brought "destruction", its policy on defence and national security, foreign policy and "neglect" of North-East, besides "undermining" of institutions including "compromising the dignity and integrity" of the office of Prime Minister.

"This government is a failure on all fronts. The legacy of UPA for a great country like India is a suffering India, insecure India, distressed India, depressed India and an India whose image stands tainted because of the shameless saga of scams and corruption.... This government will be remembered as the most corrupt government in Independent India", said BJP leader Ravi Shankar Prasad after the "chargesheet" was released. Focusing on the Congress leadership, Prasad said, "The BJP's first charge is Sonia Gandhi and Rahul Gandhi are equally guilty of all the ills in India along with Manmohan Singh, because they wanted to exercise authority without accountability," and their "deliberate, conscious devaluation" of the office of Prime Minister Manmohan Singh, who acted more like a CEO of a Board where they (Sonia and Rajiv Gandhi) had controlling interest. The BJP "chargesheet" concluded by saying, "The Congress-led UPA government has indeed been a disaster for this country. It has only left a legacy of suffering, agony, disappointment and hopelessness for the people of India. Its misdeeds in various fields have shaken the very foundation of the country."

Highlighting the "failures" of UPA on various fronts, including unfulfilled promises of 2009, BJP slammed UPA's economic policy, blamed its government of destroying every engine of Indian economy, of allowing uncontrolled inflation, declining growth rate and rising unemployment.

The next salvo was on the UPA government's responses to challenges of national security. Prasad pointed out that while on one hand the Prime Minister had declared left-wing extremists as the single biggest security threat to the country, yet the government's response has not been commensurate with the gravity and magnitude of the threat. "The soft faces of Maoist-Leftists extremist violence are having a pride of place in Sonia Gandhi's National Advisory Council," Prasad said. The BJP charge-sheet lists at least ten alleged scams of Rs 10,000 crore and more, including the 2G Spectrum, Coal mines allocation, CWG, Air India, rotten food, ISRO-Devas and Defence land scam. Besides, it also lists many other alleged scams like the Adarsh, cash-for-vote, Tatra truck, Vadra land deal, KG Basin oil scam and AgustaWestland helicopter scams. BJP said had it not been pressure from it, consistent probing by media and intervention by the court, Congress would not have ordered inquiry in any of the scams

Former Defence Minister A K Antony has been described as "the so-called honest Defence Minister is a symbol of inaction and indecision." On foreign policy matters, the UPA government has been blamed for failing to adopt an effective policy or enhance capacities of the Armed Forces to adequately meet the threat arising from China's belligerent posture along the Indo-Tibet border. "India has lost its goodwill and China's influence is increasing," he said.

Stressing that the threat from Pakistan "both overt and covert remains very serious", it said terrorists are operating against India from across the border, and infiltration and suicide attacks in Jammu and Kashmir and on sensitive security locations are continuing. Referring to the beheading of Indian soldiers near the Line of Control with Pakistan, which provoked strong outrage in the country, the party said "the requisite response was found to be wanting because of indecision of leadership." It noted that in the past two years, more than 500 incidents of border violations by Chinese troops have been reported. The UPA government failed to correctly assess military implications of these developments and take steps to shore up India's defences, the chargsheet brought out by BJP said. It failed to expedite infrastructure development work on our side of the Indo-Tibet border. Of the 503 stretches of border roads planned to be completed by the year 2022, only 17 have been completed so far and work is currently underway on just 50 stretches. It found the internal security environment deteriorating and said violence against women has caused tremendous insecurity among people. The government has "failed miserably" to check the flow of illegal immigrants to India. This despite the Supreme Court declaring it as a war against

India. Illegal immigration from Bangladesh is a major internal security concern and terrorist groups also find a ready base for furthering activities, it said. In fact, on this issue, when former Governor of Assam and Jammu and Kashmir Lt Gen S.K. Sinha, was Governor, Assam, had presented a paper to President of India bringing out how by end of 1990s, in five districts of Assam the demographical pattern had changed with illegal Bangladeshi migrants outnumbering ethnic Assamese. This writer' s book Assam Terrorism and the Demographic Challenge (Pentagon Press) published in 2009 bought out how the demographic pattern had changed similarly in eight districts. The present status of the same is believed to be of eleven districts being adversely affected.

The ironic travesty of the UPA claiming welfare of the poor while dispossessing or making them poorer, shameless land-grabbing what not else by the son-in-law of the Congress chairperson, and his derogatory jibes like "mango men" and "banana republic"—to name just a few of the misdeeds- got exposed. The allegations by India Against Corruption (IAC), as reported in The Silence of Robert Vadra, by Jatin Gandhi in open, on October 2012, read: 'In the last 4 years, Robert Vadra has gone on a property buying binge and has purchased at least 31 properties mostly in and around New Delhi, which even at the time of their purchase were worth several hundred crores. An analysis of the balance sheets and audit reports of 5 companies set up by him (and owned exclusively by him and his mother) on or after 1/11/2007 show that the total share capital of these companies was just Rs 50 lakh and these companies together had no income from any legitimate business activity (except by way of interest derived from interest free loans obtained from DLF). Yet during 2007-2010 they have acquired properties which were worth well over Rs 300 crore even at their time of acquisition and are worth more than Rs 500 crore as of today.' DLF Ltd, India's top real estate developer, issued a statement denying the charges. 'The business relationship of DLF with Mr. Robert Vadra or his companies, has been in his capacity as an individual entrepreneur, on a completely transparent and at an arm's length basis. Our business relationship has been conducted to the highest standards of ethics and transparency,' stated Sanjey Roy, vice-president, corporate

Communications, DLF, nearly 24 hours after IAC made its charges public at a press conference on 5 October in Delhi. In March 2011, when The Economic Times had reported Vadra's quiet foray into the real estate business and his association with DLF, he had told the paper, "I have known the DLF people for a long time and they are friends of mine. I had wanted to invest in real estate and one thing led to another. Right now, I can only be part of a small hotel. If I were taking favours from people I would be doing far bigger things. But I am doing this on my own. I can't expand immediately but I hope to expand a few years down the line."

The limitless grabbing of land by making an utter mockery of laws of the land and a greater mockery of the Congress party line on poverty alleviation and mocking remarks made by Vadra adversely affected the image of his wife, Priyanka and mother-in-law Sonia Gandhi and thereby Rahul Gandhi's image too. Prashad asked what the Robert Vadra model of development is—in which he began with an investment of Rs. 1 lakh and ended up making Rs. 300 crores. Priyanka Vadra reportedly referred to the BJP as "panic-stricken/baffled rats" and "vinashak, nakaratmak aur sharmnak (destructive, negative and shameful)" politics of the BJP". Such responses given not only in print but also on tv news networks not only left no doubt of what exactly was said but also indicated that there really was no explanation for their misdeeds and that they were merely responses of those drunk with power, conceit and the luxury of not being answerable.

In any case, as seen from the electioneering process and public response, Rahul Gandhi did not all seem to come anywhere near Narendra Modi. After Indira Gandhi's assassination, it was spontaneous public sympathy for Rajiv Gandhi, whose only asset was that his image was seen as quite clean and at least with enough education and qualifications to be a professional pilot. However, in the 2014 election campaigning the efforts of Sonia and Rahul Gandhi to earn sympathy by referring to the assassinations of Indira and Rajiv Gandhi, seem to have invited only criticism from the educated class at least, which in this election participated like never before by contesting as well as voting.

Another very ironic issue the Congress/UPA repeatedly rubbing against Modi was about the Godhra incident/referring to him as a 'butcher' etc. A detailed comparative study will take too much space but it must be done dispassionately and objectively and not by buying media. It should suffice to say here that figures of Sikhs killed largely in the capital and in lesser numbers in many other Indian cities/towns in punitive massacres by Congress goons led/conducted/supervised/directed by Congress leaders after Indira Gandhi's assassination, are as high as 4,733.

Having heard Mr. Narendra Modi on various issues, Mr. Rajan Arya, an experienced and astute publisher heading Pentagon Press, approached me with the idea of putting together chapters on relevant subjects from scholars and analysts for this book. Our team of writers, who have covered important issues of governance with a bias on foreign policy/diplomacy, education, women's issues and the most vital aspect-unfortunately mostly neglected and/or mismanaged so far-i.e. defence and national security. None of our team members represents any political party. We have endeavored to present the picture as a combination of our independent viewpoints and those by a cross section of people including the educated elite to the general public and not by a section of media deriving its power by being 'influenced' or plain and simple, purchased media. The mix of writers include scholars, analysts, professionals and journalists.

The Congress (in fact just the one single family—the Nehru dynasty) has been in power for almost five and a half decades of the last 67 years of independence. Over this period there is a sizeable section of print and electronic media which, ranging from subtly to most obviously, has been projecting the Congress even at the cost of the essential principle of free media- of presenting the true picture.

While there is no doubt about Narendra Modi's leadership qualities, astuteness, statesmanship, scientific temper, administrative capability, a sense of history and other attributes, this book is merely a humble attempt at bringing out what should have been done since independence, but was not done and what should be done in the near future, for much needed progress and improvement in certain key fields of governance.

CONTRIBUTORS

Siva Sivapragasa is the Editor of "Monsoon Journal" which is being published from Canada.

PDT Achary, is a former Secretary General of Lok Sabha. He spent 40 years in his service of Parliament and has contributed greatly in strengthening of the instrumentalities of Parliament.

Lt Col Anil Bhat, VSM (Retd), served in the infantry and armoured corps. Specially selected for public affairs with Defence Ministry, he pioneered in India's North Eastern region raising two new offices of the Ministry in Manipur and Assam during intensive phases of insurgency and terrorism and later posted as the Indian Army spokesperson in Delhi. A former Research Fellow at Institute for Defence Studies & Analyses, member of four prestigious think tanks, he has written extensively on national and South Asian security / terrorism, military history and defence industry. A syndicated columnist with articles and book reviews in many newspapers and magazines as well as research papers in many edited books and journals, he is Editor, WordSword Features, Associate Editor, Salute Magazine, Consulting Editor, The Diplomatist magazine, author of three books and is fluent in four Indian languages.

Maj Gen (Dr) G D Bakshi SM, VSM (Retd) is the quintessential Scholar-warrior. A PHD in Strategic studies, he has authored 26 books and over 150 papers. A Member of many prestigious think tanks, he appears regularly on national TV debates. Currently, he is Editor Indian Military Review and Senior Advisor with the Reliance Industries Ltd.

Talmiz Ahmad, joined the Indian Foreign Service in 1974, and served as Indian Ambassador to Saudi Arabia (2000-03; 2010-11); Oman (2003-04), and the UAE (2007-10). Additional Secretary for International Cooperation in the Ministry of Petroleum and Natural Gas (2004-06) and Director General, Indian Council of World Affairs, New Delhi (2006-07), he has authored two books. Presently he is working with an energy company in Dubai and is a Visiting Distinguished Fellow at Observer Research Foundation.

Dr Sudhir Singh has done his PhD from Jawaharlal Nehru University, New Delhi. He has enormously contributed on national and human rights issues. He is presently teaching in the department of political science, Dyal Singh College, University of Delhi, New Delhi.

Dr Pankaj K Jha is Research Fellow with Indian Council of World Affairs (ICWA). Prior to that he was the Deputy Director with National Security Council Secretariat (2012-13), Prime Minister's Office.

Sudipt Arora is Director, Content Management and Media Planning, at Avian Media—a communications consultancy practice.

Tripti Nath is a second generation journalist. In a career spanning 21 years, she has worked for *The Sunday Times*, London, the French Embassy, *The Tribune*, *The Pioneer*, *The Asian Age* and *The Statesman*. At present, she is working for *The Asahi Shimbun*, Japan's leading national daily.

Sheetal Jain is an author and educator. She is running project called as School of Humanism in various schools in Delhi and around where she trains Students, parents and teachers on Life Values. For last 5 years she has been organizing workshops for same in different schools of Delhi. She wants to merge spiritual education into main education system, so that we can create a stronger individual and a stronger society.

Dr Suresh R, Associate Professor, Department of Political Science, University of Kerala, Kariavattom, Kerala.

Ruchi Ramesh is teaching in the department of Sociology, R.K.M.V. Shimla. As a researcher she has delved deep into the social issues that beset diverse sections of society including Tribes and Human rights.

Piyush Tiwari is Founder and CEO, SaveLIFE Foundation, an advocacy group, which aims to reduce the high number of road accident deaths in India through rapid emergency care for injured victims. It is also working to create a supportive legal framework for bystanders to help victims of accidents and other trauma. It filed two Public Interest Litigations in the Hon'ble Supreme Court of India in order to address gaps in the current scenario dealing with road safety.

1

The Beginning of the Modi Era

Siva Sivapragasam

Narendra Modi has become the Prime Minister of India, world's largest democracy, at a time when the country is desperate for a change in leadership and regime. As a career politician he has led his party through an invigorating, high-tech election campaign. The people who voted him to power will now naturally look forward for results.

The Congress party's rule over the last few years has been looked upon as a decade of decay. Modi's criticism of the Congress rule was based on the corruption scandals, rise in prices, a weak foreign policy and family politics. These allegations combined and contributed to the downfall of the Congress. Narendra Modi's success as a Prime Minister and effective leader will therefore depend on how he will tackle the issues of criticism he levelled against Congress.

It was Modi's mix of economic efficiency and hardline nationalism that mesmerized the voters in India with a "Modi Wave" when they were looking for a change of leadership and Government. Modi enjoys massive support among India's middle classes and business community who credit him with turning Gujarat into an economic powerhouse. One would therefore expect Modi to satisfy the aspirations of these groups. It is stated that foreign investors have pumped in over Rupees one lakh crore in the Indian securities market since Narendra Modi was announced as the Prime Ministerial candidate by the Bharatiya

Janata Party (BJP) in September last year. This is an indication of the trust he has created among the investing groups. Hinduja Group Chairman Srichand Hinduja has described Narendra Modi's massive mandate as a vote for stability that will put India back on the path of high growth. Hinduja Group is one of the largest diversified business groups in the world. Modi's image has been looked upon and approved as a leader who can offer a stable government. He should therefore tap the resources of foreign investment to the maximum bearing in mind that it should not cut into the efforts of the local business sector. Diversifying the economy to allow foreign companies to enter the market by themselves or with a majority stake, will of course be controversial. But, it may also be the sensible step India's new government can take to keep the economic engine running.

If India is to achieve a global power status it should focus its attention towards improvement and development of the infrastructure in the country. India needs tremendous spurt towards the improvement of its roads, railways and public utilities. It should attempt to remove restrictions and hurdles from implementation of such projects. Red-tape has to be eliminated so as to quicken developmental efforts of investors and business groups. Mr Modi's success in this front has been witnessed in Gujarat when the Tata Motors and Ford have both cited his successful policy to cut down bureaucracy and red-tape as the main reasons they moved their Indian operating bases to Gujarat. Infrastructure development, real estate investment and tourism have grown under Modi's administration in Gujarat, as has the agricultural sector through public-private partnerships. He has experimented a lot in Gujarat. In the report by the US Congressional Research Service (CRS), Gujarat has been declared as the state having the most effective governance under the leadership of Modi. Currently, he is the only person who can implement his experience to the rest of the nation. It can be expected that India will be a totally different country after few years under the leadership of Modi. Some of the developmental plans may have short-term goals while others may have long-term goals. In a nation that is desperately looking for changes the mood is to see results soon and Modi has to bear that in mind.

It has been said that Modi does not depend on others for decision making. Those who have worked with him say that he takes in inputs from others but makes his own decision. His promise of development, job opportunities, clean and corruption free administration and good governance had won over even those who doubted his capability. Apart from the role the state is expected to play he will have to enlist the private sector to share the responsibility of development and growth. This, he can achieve by providing incentives and creating a sense of trust and confidence for the investors.

Delegation of power and devolution to his deputies and co-opting state leaders to attain his goals of development will help accelerate his visions of growth. The need for finances for his developmental efforts would also mean looking out for revenue measures to increase the State coffers.

The underlying theme of Modi's speeches at election meetings was based on the economic development of India combined with attacks on a corrupted government, weak leadership and dynasty politics. The speeches in the campaign trail suggested that he will now seek to govern in a way that will spurt economic growth, create job opportunities and improve infrastructure, along with further reductions in poverty and inflation. Modi kept emphasizing the need for a strong government to achieve this. The voters were convinced that a Modi Government will improve their material lives. Mr Modi has been dropping strong hints that he hopes to remain in power not only for the current five-year term, but to win re-election and reshape India's economy and political landscape. In other words, he is considering his long-term prospects by keeping in mind the rise of a powerful new nation that will gain more recognition and influence in the years to come. It is likely that Modi will offer a priority measure to attract foreign investment. BJP spokespersons have also hinted that the party still may reverse an existing policy that would allow foreign investors to open supermarkets in larger cities, under limited circumstances. He may well think of attracting more foreign capital into a variety of sectors which could include insurance, banking, defence and many sections of infrastructure development. He needs to send a clear message when he begins to offer policy that India aspires to become strong on the back of economic growth, more international trade, deeper global engagement—and not by promoting nationalist tendencies at home. He has a decent record of reaching out to other countries, notably Japan, in his time as Chief Minister of Gujarat. Modi needs to balance nationalism of a protectionist variety with attracting foreign investment. Since his victory on 16 May he has fielded calls from Barack Obama, David Cameron and a host of other global well-wishers eager to engage India internationally. Fareed Zackaria, CNN's Political Correspondent has described Modi as "authoritative and a quick decision maker" who turned the state of Gujarat into one of India's most reputed powerhouse. These natural qualities of leadership and decision making should be an asset to him in his new role as a Prime Minister of the country.

BJP is not well represented in the Upper House and Modi must be able to convince members that his programme of action and plans he envisages are for the betterment of India's future. He has successfully established a name that he can turn things around with the Gurajat experiment. He must capitalize on this and instil hope and trust among the people. It is expected that the PMO (Prime Minister's Office) will play a central role in decision-making on important issues including national security and direct supervision of critical infrastructure projects and administrative reforms. Mr. Modi's PMO could emerge as a more powerful body than any previous institution. His well-laid out plans centre on creating a framework which would allow the Prime Minister's Office to fast-track decisions. It is also likely that he would rely on some of his trusted administrative staff in Gujarat to be co-opted into the PMO's office. He will have to empower the PMO with more direct involvement in decision-making. Bureaucrats and technocrats should be encouraged for faster decision-making.

Some of the key-ministries such as finance, external affairs and energy may have to be re-structured. Although he is democratically elected, Modi is authoritarian in style and spirit. Many feel that the future of India's development belongs to Narendra Modi. Internationally reputed *Time Magazine* once referred Modi in it's front cover as "Modi Means Business". The success of Narendra Modi will be judged only by a historic innings followed by a historic win. He has also maintained strong links with the conservative Hindu nationalist group, Rashtriya Swayamsevak Sangh or RSS. "The RSS will have a substantial check on Modi. He is not going to be entirely his own man," says political analyst Kamal Mitra Chenoy of the Jawaharlal Nehru University, New Delhi.

"The kind of hope he's aroused is unprecedented. He'll have to deliver very quickly," says political analyst Neerja Chowdhury.

Many say that Modi's success comes down to his ability to connect with the common man. He repeatedly has emphasized his origins outside New Delhi and outside the country's elite classes. Mr. Modi has established himself as a leader of unquestionable integrity. He has set very high expectations for economic revival and good governance. He has focused his entire energy on building Gujarat with an able administration and good governance. He has achieved phenomenal development and economic growth. He can achieve these goals for the whole of India only if he gets complete support from all sections of the population and avoid sectarian divisions. He has set a good tone by promising to work for the good of all Indians, and he will need to stick to that commitment. An advantage Modi has is that he will have a confidence in what he does because of the absolute majority he enjoys in Parliament. It is expected that he will work for the welfare of India and keep clear of communal politics or minority politics. Everyone is bound to benefit in his model of governance. He has a vision of creating hundreds of new cities in India. His unique style and spirit of governance which one had seen in Gujarat makes one believe that he will achieve the goals he has in mind. He provided a very accountable, transparent and clean government in Gujarat. With his leadership qualities and experience it is expected that he will present a similar picture as Prime Minister of India.

2

For a Meaningful Engagement with Parliament

P D T Achary

Shri Narendra Damodardas Modi became the prime minister of India after a two months long election ordeal which also saw the decimation of the former ruling party, the Indian National Congress (I). Never in the history of India has a political leader, that too the priministerial candidate of the principal opposition party, had to suffer the kind of insults and innuendoes which Shri Modi had to suffer ever since he occupied the central space in national politics about two years ago. Political leaders, big and small, intellectuals, media and even non-political beings from political families revelled in hurling invectives at him ostensibly because of his non elitist background and a perceived ineligibility to run this "complex country". The 16th general elections will be remembered for long for the new benchmarks it established in abusive and acrimonious election campaigns. But it is indeed a riddle to most of India's politicians, political pundits and others of their ilk that the people remained unswayed by the fulminations of the invective-hurling political class and voted for a stable government and a person to lead it whom they took seriously.

It is very interesting and also amusing to see the leaders of parties which have been trounced by the people struggling to find the reasons for their loss. Political organisations which are supposed to be always in touch with the people should know why they lost. Here lies the problem. It is our common experience that the political leaders who come to power start moving away from the people and their concerns the moment they take office. Slowly the corporates, bureaucrats, the personal assistance, sundry power brokers and above all the army of sycophants filled their mental space and gradually began guiding them. Further, arrogance about their political high office crept in drove out concerns of ordinary people. Their busy schedules left no time for ordinary people's problems and aspirations. Finally the election results rudely wake them up to the reality and make them wonder what went wrong and why.

Shri Narendra Modi is one political leader who knew what was happening. An intellectual with roots in the BJP told me that Shri Modi knew about three years ago that the government which has been voted out was going to meet this fate and started his campaign in right earnest. This was possible because he was in touch with the people and their problems. The people were angry with the government because it had only increased their miseries and at the end of five years they had nothing to look forward to. Shri Modi reached out to them and promised to change the situation and assured them a better life. Thus India witnessed a mass mobilisation the like of which it has rarely seen. In this mobilisation Modi became the theme, the message, and the messenger. Conservative political pundits complained of a personality cult which they said was against democracy. They forgot that the personality of the leader was central to Indian democracy. That the absence of a strong personality brings disaster has been proved by the previous government.

India's democratic system made it possible for a person with humble beginnings to become the prime minister. Shri Modi has internalised this dimension of our democracy. When he knelt down and touched his forehead to the ground at the entry gate of parliament house while entering the building for the first time he was conveying a powerful message to the entire nation that parliament is a sacred place and that he will always preserve and protect its sanctity. The powerful symbolism of this gesture has awakened the deepest patriotic feelings in the Indian mind. Modi's appeal and message have an irresistibility about them.

The centrality of parliament in our system establishes the sovereignty of people. India's experiment in democracy based on universal adult franchise was by all accounts unprecedented for a country steeped in poverty and illiteracy and grave social inequalities. But elections during the past 62 years have strengthened the roots of democracy and this experiment has made India the largest function democracy in the world.

India's parliament is a very vibrant representative body which has guided the destiny of our life and is a proud symbol of our nationhood. It is in this forum the government is held accountable. In fact the image of a government is made and unmade here. As a watch dog of the nation's interests parliament looks into the government's actions with a sharp eye and cautions, corrects and chastises it when it does wrong. Parliament legislates and passes the budget. No money can be appropriated without the authority of parliament. Every pie the government spends is scrutinised by parliament. Every action, every omission and commission has to be explained before it. Parliament can also refuse to sanction money if it feels that the government is not acting in the interest of the people.

Such is the extent of powers of parliament in our constitutional scheme free India's parliament established robust systems for its functioning which enhanced its reputation as the supreme legislature as well as the watch dog of public interest. The leaders who led the nation in the formative years of the Republic took great care to strengthen the system by laying down rules and guide lines and conventions. Great parliamentarians who are remembered always for there contributions to parliament nurtured healthy traditions and conventions and strengthened the supervisory structures of parliament. Thus parliament had effective control over the executive which is central to the parliamentary system.

However over a period of time the effectiveness of this great institution has eroded. A variety of factors have contributed to this state of affairs. The highly personalised and adversarial politics of the 1970s gave rise to a tendency to give less importance to parliament which came to be regarded as a nuisance by the rulers. The prime minister would think nothing much of the opposition who had no trust in the former. In fact there was a debilitating enmity between the government and the opposition. The speaker who is required to uphold the majesty of parliament would have to look over his shoulder before a decision was taken to admit or disallow motions against the government. Prime minister Nehru on the other hand used to sit in parliament most of the time during the session and intervene whenever he thought necessary. He used to supplement replies the questions given by his ministers. That tradition was given up and a new tradition of the prime minister avoiding the Houses of parliament as much as possible came to be established and which continued till recently.

The parliament did not function during the past three to four years. A kind of chaos had overtaken it. The government watched the disruption day in and day absolutely unconcerned and not interested in taking any meaningful initiative to break the stalemate. This attitude of the government was in a sense at the root of the malfunctioning of parliament. There was a complete breakdown of the system. At the end of the fifteenth Lok Sabha, over sixty bills—most of them very important—lapsed on the dissolution of Lok Sabha. In the mean time an attempt was made to promulgate ordinances which did not succeed reportedly because of opposition from Rashtrapati Bhawan.

Disruption of parliament was the most visible sign of the malfunctioning of the system. But more serious systemic problems have emerged which have never attracted the attention of the principal stake holders. The most powerful supervisory structure of parliament consists of the parliamentary committees which are meant to scrutinise every act of the executive and ensure its accountability to parliament. When we compare the working of the committees of today with those of the earlier days we find how deep rot has gone. The hard work put in by the members in studying the voluminous material supplied by the ministries, the well planned and well coordinated questioning of officials and the guidance given by the chairman to the members to facilitate the questioning of government officials made the committees the most effective instruments for truth finding. The most crucial aspect of the committee system was that the committees functioned on absolutely non partisan lines and there was unanimity of views on all major issues. This healthy and time honoured tradition is slowly being jettisoned now, jeopardizing the system of parliamentary scrutiny. Today the scrutiny by committees is mostly perfunctory with most of the members showing less interest and some, no interest at all. Being nominated to the committees without ascertaining their area of interest, many of them are like square pegs in round holes. Even then, if they develop sufficient interest in a subject they can acquire special knowledge about it in course of time but the members of parliament have no time or inclination to take the committees' work seriously. Their world and activities are limited to their constituencies. They have to attend funerals, marriages, naming and feeding ceremonies of children important people in their constituencies and a whole lot of other activities unrelated to parliament.

They fear that if they fail to do all this the people will not vote for them next time. These are the main concerns of an average member of Lok Sabha. Attending funerals or marriages is more important for many of them than attending parliament. How can they then take the parliamentary work seriously? On most of the occasions they come into the committee rooms straight from the airport without reading the agenda or the background material. The only people who are happy about this situation are the officials from various ministries because they won't have to face any tough questioning by the members. The reports of the committees are prepared by the employees of the secretariat. The quality of the reports depends wholly on the ability of these employees to comprehend the subject matter. The contribution of individual members in the formulation of recommendations is virtually nonexistent.

The speaker has a major role in maintaining the health of the system. The deterioration in the working of committees is attributable to a great extent to the lack of interest or indifference show by many speakers in the past with the exception of Shri Somnath chatterjee. The fifteenth Lok Sabha witnessed a precipitous decline and the whole system almost came to a grinding halt. What happened in the JPC and PAC was horrendous, with the chairman of JPC on 2G scam creating history of sorts by refusing to hear the principal accused in the scam. He finalised the report without hearing him, which is unheard of in any system of investigation. The open division and procedural monstrosity which took place in the PAC is well known. But there was no intervention by the speaker at any time to normalise the working of these important committees although the rules of the House mandate the speaker to set things right.

A key functionary of the government who can help to resolve the conflicts arising in the Houses of parliament is the minister for parliamentary affairs (MPA). Though this ministry does not enjoy any high profile its task of coordinating the work in the two houses is of tremendous importance. The MPA is the bridge between the government and opposition and an MPA in whom the opposition has intrinsic faith is the best minister. There were a few legendary MPAs in the past but one who stands out is the Late Shri K Raghuramayya. He is undoubtly the role model for all MPAs. Though Indira Gandhi had two-thirds majority in the fifth Lok Sabha, Raghuramayya would be seen mostly on the opposition benches, sitting with them coaxing and cajoling them to have a smooth running of the house. Indira Gandhi had an innate distrust of the opposition. Raghuramayya with his silver tongue and friendly ways could easily win them over. Because of his frequent presence on the opposition benches, an opposition leader once jokingly told the treasury benches "Look your parliamentary affairs minister has defected to our side." Much of the problem which bedevilled the fifteenth Lok Sabha was due in a large measure to the absence of a tactful, wise and suave MPA who could build bridges between the government and the opposition. For the old parliament watchers it was a horrifying experience to see the MPA shouting abuses at the opposition to impress his leader sitting in the front row of the treasury benches. No wonder the houses did not function most of the time.

The present ruling party has an absolute majority on its own and with its allies is comfortably placed in the Lok Sabha. It is led by a Prime Minister who is decisive and firm and has demonstrated his emotional and almost reverential attachment to parliament. The ruling party has some of the country's senior most parliamentarians within its ranks. With this asset it won't be very difficult for the government to address the problem of the enfeeblement of the system and take steps to revitalise it. The speaker, Smt Sumitra Mahajan is one of the senior most members of the House and is conversant with the strengths and weaknesses of the system. She has the right credentials to reform it. Shri Venkayya Naidu, the new MPA is a senior political leader who has the stature and political maturity to keep the relationship between the government and the opposition at a congenial level. Even at the worst of times the dialogue between the government and the opposition has to go on. Further, the presence of the prime minister in the house and his active engagement with it can solve any difficult problem that may arise there. The prime minister with his hands on approach can channelize the enormous energy of the house into constructive debates on issues of importance and in strengthening the systems of parliament. The prime minister can interact with members of parliament as often as he can in, for example, the Bureau of Parliamentary Studies and Training (BPST), an institution under the secretariat of the house of the people and share his thoughts with them. Such frequent interactions between the prime minister and the Members of parliament will reduce the distance between the latter and the government, create confidence among the members and in the capacity and willingness of the government to respond to issues. And above all, the prime minister will get a firsthand knowledge of what is happening in the country. There should also be attempts to encourage specialisation among the MPs who have the aptitude for certain fields, like external affairs, defence, science and technology, environment etc. In fact, MPs should be helped to acquire specialisation in those subjects. Every parliament in the world except India's has such groups of MP's who have specialised in various subjects. In international conferences this lack of specialisation seriously affects the performance and utility of our MP's. An institutional arrangement exists in the Lok Sabha in the name of Parliamentary Forums started by Speaker Chatterjee. These forums remained dormant during the last Lok Sabha as the speaker of that house did not know what to do with them. These forums can be activated to impart specialisation in different subjects. Such specialisation will ultimately enhance the level and quality of debates in the houses. The level of debate on external affairs and defence particularly, was abysmally poor in the last few Lok Sabhas because MP's did not have in-depth knowledge about these vital areas. With 315 young MP's in the new Lok Sabha it would be in the interest of the institution of parliament to train them to be good debaters. If their youthful energy and enthusiasm is allowed to go waste it will be a permanent loss to the institution.

Our parliament evokes pride in us. It represents the past and the future. It has a glorious past. It legislated for bringing social revolution. Men of great wisdom adorned its benches. Its walls echoed the vibrant voices of great orators, giants who were respected by the whole world. It witnessed and became instrumental in the march of the nation towards progress and prosperity. Today a generational change has taken place in its chamber. The prime minister can easily connect with this new generation and take them along with him in his journey to fulfil inspirational India's dreams. The chamber of the house should reverberate with their voice—the voice of young India full of hope and a passion for change.

3

Challenges for Narendra Modi on National Security and Related Foreign Policy

Anil Bhat

An Overview

India attained independence after centuries of being attacked, marauded, pillaged, converted and ruled over. Being very geo-strategically located, having just gone through the unprecedented ordeal of partition, India had already acquired one hostile neighbour on two of its extremities. There was another big neighbour, whose intentions with indications on the ground should have been assessed properly. It was a crucial stage for taking some hard decisions and formulating policies which would keep this large nation secure and integrated and also make it strong and prosperous to not only hold its own, but also to be able to influence its large, diverse, and to a great extent, inimical neighbourhood. However, unfortunately, that was not to be and India's political leadership made a very poor start by (a) failing to study the nature and extent of India's vast land and sea boundaries; (b) failing to realise the importance of military muscle and the timely use of adequate/ appropriate force; (c) being ignorant/naïve about tendencies/intentions of neighbours like China and Pakistan; (d) looking at the armed forces with suspicion and creating phobia of military rule; (e) developing/ propagating a warped sense of secularism by obliterating history and (f) laying the foundation of sycophancy, dynastic politics and corruption.

It should be noted that a major factor of the timing and hastening of the exit of the British was the Indian army. It was 1.5 million Indian troops in World War I and 2.5 million in World War II who made the decisive contribution to allied victories in both these wars. The reputation of Indian soldiers worldwide then was that of being fearless and highly professional. When the Indian Navy personnel mutinied, the British were badly shaken. They realised to their consternation what the consequences could be if that mutiny spread to the much larger 2.5 million strong Indian Army. It was that factor which made them leave in a hurry. During the first India-Pakistan war in 1947-48 the British were like unfair referees, quite partial to Pakistan.

Unfortunately, India's political leadership holding the centre-stage at that time decided to look at such an army with suspicion and, sad to say, that the then prime minister and defence minister went out of their way to not only ignore any sound advice from the army, but also meddled with the army's leadership, with disastrous results like the 1962 Chinese aggression, when this same professional army obeying the orders of the government as per norms of a democracy, had to fight under-armed, ill-equipped and insufficiently clad and suffered a humiliating defeat.

In dealing with Pakistan during the first war it had already perpetrated with Independence, no aggressive use of the air force was made and the navy was not even utilised. During the Chinese aggression again no aggressive use of the air force was made. During the second India-Pakistan war of 1965, the navy was completely kept out of the loop and the then naval chief ironically visited the operational area as an observer, even as Pakistan navy launched an attack, albeit unsuccessfully.

The only exceptions of assertiveness against inimical neighbours/ external attacks in over six decades since Independence were by Shrimati Indira Gandhi.

In 1967, when Chinese army upped the ante at Nathu La in Sikkim by repeated firing of not only small arms but also artillery, resulting in a number of fatal casualties the brigade commander requested for sanction to respond with artillery. She promptly accorded the sanction. The response resulted in about 400 Chinese soldiers being killed and a number of Chinese vehicles and fortifications being destroyed. The message that 1962 cannot be repeated was effectively sent to the Chinese. Since then, despite many confrontations and incursions by Chinese troops on the Line of Actual Control, no bullets have been exchanged between Chinese and Indian forces.

During the build-up towards the 1971 Indo-Pak war, Shrimati Gandhi heard and heeded the advice of the Army Chief and following a well-planned operation on two major fronts, with very effective use of the navy for the first time, resulting in not only Pakistan's defeat yet again, but also the liberation of Bangladesh. The US sending its 7th Fleet also did not make her lose any sleep. However, where she faltered at last was during the Simla talks, when she fell for Zulfikar Bhutto's dramatics and lies and by not using the 12,000 sq km of Pakistan's territory in the Western sector as major bargaining chip of 'Land for Peace'.

Handling of Jammu and Kashmir (J&K) leaves much to be desired. The government in late 1980s failed to protect Kashmiri Pandits from the diabolical designs of Pakistan's army/Inter Services Intelligence and further failed to prevent their exodus from the Kashmir valley. More failures followed in responding to the fourth war by Pakistan, which is continuing in some form or the other till date. India's action against the Kargil intrusion in 1999 was only about six months late as Pak army raised 12 battalions of Northern Light Infantry, which began crossing the Line of Control (LoC) in 1998 itself, when Musharraf was DG, Military Operations.

Since the 1993 bombings in Mumbai (before which the relationship between ISI and Dawood Ibrahim and his Mumbai underworld underlings had got cemented), attack on Parliament, 26/11 terrorist attack by ISI, LeT, al-Qaeda etc., on Mumbai, or the 2013 attacks across the LoC and across the International Boundary—all went un-retaliated, or at least, not appropriately enough. Pakistan very well understands the language of without-fail-retaliation of any military or terrorist attack and also of India being able to strike at terrorist leaders who motivate the masses at Muridke, Karachi, Lahore or anywhere else in Pakistan, if India's decision-makers decide to do so. Such retaliation requires not only Indian Army's quick and unrestrained responses on the LoC or the International Boundary, but also of a very effective covert cross-border strike capability.

The North East stands out as a combination of ignorance, neglect and mishandling. While only the Mizo accord is an exception, in Manipur, Nagaland and Assam problems related to insurgencies converted to terrorism, thanks to impetus and arms provided by ISI from Bangladesh since the 1990s.

In both Manipur and Nagaland, the militant-terrorist National Socialist Council of Nagaland/Nagalim-Isaac-(NSCN-IM) group has its presence. A ceasefire between security forces and NSCN-IM has been in effect since 15 August 1997 and talks between this group and Government of India have been carrying on. What is most unusual about this ceasefire and talks is that the NSCN-IM was not made to lay down arms. This group has made a mockery of both the ceasefire and the talks, as it continues to run a parallel government in both these states by continuing extortion in the name of 'taxes', abductions, murder and even treachery, as it has links with Pakistan's ISI and Chinese intelligence, through which it is acquiring arms and ammunition and supplying the same to Naxal-Maoists. Yet, the Centre continues talks with NSCN-IM.

In Manipur there are a number of militant-terrorist Meitei groups which are also involved in extortion, murders and have links with ISI and Chinese intelligence, as well as with some political leaders.

What has happened in Assam is indeed a matter of great concern. The terrorist group, United Liberation Front of Asom (ULFA) rose from the Assam agitation of 1983 on the issue of entry and migration of foreigners (erstwhile East Pakistanis and post-1971, Bangladeshis) into Assam. When the Army was launched against it in 1990, its senior leaders under Paresh Barua escaped to Bangladesh, from where they came under control of the ISI (which had a major presence there during regimes of Bangladesh Nationalist Party). It was the ULFA which facilitated the entry of ISI into India's North Eastern states and its contact with other terrorist groups in that region, thereby providing the ISI with the Eastern pincer. Not only that, it facilitated the entry and settling of Bangladeshi illegal migrants to such a level that today there are 11 districts of Assam which have undergone demographic shifts with Bangladeshi Muslims outnumbering ethnic Assamese people. When Lt Gen S K Sinha was Governor of Assam, he submitted a paper to President of India in 1998, warning that at least 5 districts of Assam had undergone this demographic shift. In a book titled Assam Terrorism and the Demographic Challenge, which I wrote in 2008, I brought out that 8 districts had undergone the demographic change. This change was also facilitated by Assamese Congress ministers, who generously dished out ration cards to Bangladeshi migrants to enhance their vote-banks. When Awami League came back to power in Bangladesh with a thumping majority in end of 2008, it rounded up some senior ULFA leaders enjoying sanctuary in Bangladesh and returned them to India, where they were put in jails. Chief Minister Shri Tarun Gogoi had them freed in the name of talks, which are continuing with the Centre. Paresh Barua escaped from Bangladesh to Myanmar, from where he keeps shuttling to China. Whereas he now heads the so-called anti-talks faction, there is contact between him and the so-called pro-talks ULFA leaders, who were freed from Jails by Shri Gogoi at such a time that they could 'influence' (read threaten) Assamese voters to vote for Shri Gogoi, who like earlier, got elected back to power for the third time.

Naxal-Maoists have spread to so many districts creating a Red Corridor, mainly because all states affected are not on the same page as far as effective counter-measures against them are concerned.

Many of India's internal security problems have become externally linked. However, the fact remains that a very major factor in effectively fighting them has its genesis in the failure to implement police reforms, which Supreme Court has strongly recommended. India is out of those countries with a very low policeman-to-population ratio. State and central police forces need to be modernised. Particularly state police forces need a total make-over. Police reforms as such must be speedily implemented.

It took an attack like 26/11 on Mumbai for the country to wake up to the urgent and pressing requirement of coastal police in all coastal states. This task is still on but needs great impetus of manpower and resources.

There are many other points and issues related to national security, which space does not permit to elaborate upon.

Today we are caught in a web of vote-bank/twisted secularism politics, in which our key leaders are vying to score self-goals on national security and refusing to straightening their spines to maintain this hard won independence after ten centuries of being marauded, converted by the sword and ruled. Meanwhile as we lose more trained soldiers and innocent citizens alike, we seem to be fated to hope that we finally elect a government which will at least not compromise on national security.

Should Pacts of Peace and Acts of War Go Together?

Coinciding with the September 25-28, 2012 India-US dialogue in Washington DC and sinisterly timed with PM Manmohan Singh's "on the sidelines" meeting with his Pakistani counterpart, came yet another multi-target attack by highly trained Pakistani terrorists in J&K. US President Barack Obama's statement during the dialogue that there is a worldwide terror threat from Pakistan-based groups also turned out to be ominous because this time, after a long gap since 2002, Pakistani terrorists came across the International Boundary in the plains stretch of South J&K, striking at Hiranagar and Samba. Their aim was of not merely repeating 15 May 2002-attack at Indian Army's family quarters complex at Kalu Chak, but surpassing it by attacking the Army School at Samba, after attacking 16th Cavalry. The timing of this attack, like the one in Kalu Chak, was in the morning when personnel have returned from first parade for breakfast and change of uniform for second parade and children are getting ready for school. In the Kalu Chak attack a total of 31 were killed: 3 Army personnel, 18 Army family members including 10 children and 10 civilians. 47 were wounded including 12 Army personnel, 20 Army family members and 15 civilians. In this attack, 4 personnel were killed as all ranks of 16th Cavalry-commanding officer downwards and the brigade swung into action and finally killed the three terrorists, who would have escaped and launched more surprise attacks.

On the Patahankot-Jammu national highway (NH 1A), the 22-km stretch between Kathua, Hiranagar and Samba is more or less parallel to the International Boundary between India and Pakistan and about 15 km away from it. The army units of Samba are strewn on both sides of the highway.

On 26 September 2013, the 3 terrorists very advantageously dressed in Indian Army battle fatigues, reportedly first charged into the Hiranagar police station at about 6.45 am and lobbing a grenade indiscriminately fired from their AK-47, killing an Assistant Sub-Inspector (ASI), 3 constables and a civilian and injuring another ASI. The terrorists thereafter hijacked a tempo truck on the highway, boarded it and forced its driver to move towards Jammu. Approaching Samba, they headed for the entrance gate of 16th Cavalry (the very first unit on the right side of the road), immediately fired on the sentry and rushed inside the premises.

Eventually, all three terrorists were killed, while 16th Cavalry lost Lt Col Bikramjit Singh, Dafadar Inder Singh of the mess staff and Sowars Kiran Kumar and M S Rao. The CO, Col Avin Uthaiya was seriously injured. At Hiranagar the final death count was 8.

These two attacks form part of a definite pattern emerging from the beginning of 2013, i.e. intrusion and beheading, intrusion and killing 5 Indian soldiers (4 of them from 24 Bihar), intrusion of a large body of Pak army troops with terrorists in Keran sector-all three along the Line of Control (LoC) and intrusion across the International Boundary to launch attacks at Hiranagar and Samba. Then there have been a series of attacks by Pakistani terrorists in Srinagar itself. There were some indicators of such ratcheting-up in 2012 itself. The intrusions vis-a-vis firing across the LoC and IB in J&K and that too by 'battle action teams'—a combo of special Pak army troops and terrorists, are not mere "skirmishes", as reportedly referred to by both External Affairs Minister Salman Khurshid and J&K CM Omar Abdullah. They are acts of war, like the 26/11 attack in Mumbai was. What are as disturbing as the attacks are the government's reactions and various statements from India's top political leaders. Pakistan's high commissioner Salman Bashir denials and lies should not at all be surprising.

Mr. Khurshid said in New York that the twin terror attacks in J&K will not derail talks between India and Pakistan. "There is no alternative. There are forces that do not want the India-Pakistan situation to be normalised. If we succumb (to these forces) we are playing into Satan's hands. The roots of the event will have to be addressed, and that will need some kind of engagement with our neighbour," Mr Khurshid is reported to have stated on the sidelines of a UN meeting. India is evaluating the evidence that the three terrorists who carried out the attacks in J&K were from Pakistan, Mr Khurshid said, "Once our side is clear about what happened, we will speak to our Pakistani counterparts...we know that there is infrastructure that encourages, supports and organises such attacks. But countries talk via established governments. And especially since Mr Sharif was democratically elected by the Pakistani people who also want him to serve that mandate".

What does Mr. Khurshid have to say about the perpetrators of terror like Hafiz Saeed and some thousands of terrorists motivated by him and his cohorts, walking free in Pakistan, waiting to attack India? And who is the Indian government trying to impress with its misplaced restraint/disastrous soft approach? The government must realise that its reactions and statements send wrong messages to the adversary, to the global community, to the country, and worse, to those guarding its integrity. A number of retired army veterans with long years of experience on the LoC and Pak army's modus operandi are very apprehensive about this soft approach, which they stress is confusing and worse, demoralising for soldiers bearing the brunt of cease fire violations and attacks across the LoC, border men guarding the IB.

Speaking to *The Asian Age*, Army Chief Gen Bikram Singh did not pull any punches. He reiterated that infiltrations along the LoC are being supported by Pakistan Army and clearly confirmed what this writer has stated in this newspaper's earlier columns that they are expected to continue and become increasingly desperate, as there are many trained and motivated terrorists waiting in launching pads across the LoC. Adding that such intrusions cannot but be without Pak army's support he stressed that Northern Command fully anticipates and is prepared for this trend and that its field commanders are giving appropriate responses. The ratcheting up by Pak army is also because of desperation resulting from many failed attempts to push in infiltrating terrorists across the LoC owing to the fencing and aggressive guarding by Indian Army. While Pak army chief Gen Ashfaq Pervez Kayani's statement that Indian military's comments are provocative, it is not surprising at all. His latest rabbit out of the hat is that United Nations should investigate incidents on the LoC.

The Research and Analysis Wing (RAW) is reported to have informed the government about Hafiz Saeed visiting Pakistan-occupied Kashmir for giving final shape to the phase of terrorist operations after withdrawal of American forces from Afghanistan of hordes of *mujahideen* being inducted across the border into India for renewing "*jihad*" in Kashmir. The RAW report also categorically states that there have been attempts by terror groups to carry out strikes against the "vulnerable off-duty men" of the security forces.

New Delhi's politico-diplomatic responses must be appropriate and backed with adequate timely retaliations on the borders. Also, the capability for effective covert actions well beyond our borders must be honed pronto.

According to information given by Defence Minister Shri A K Antony in a written reply to Shri N Balaganga in Rajya Sabha on 18 December 2013, there were 93 ceasefire violations (CFVs) along the Line of Control in J&K during 2012 and 196 in 2013 (till 15 December 2013).

India's Threshold of Restraint on its Borders

A large number of violations of the LoC by Pakistan army and also very many unusual intrusions across the Line of Actual Control (LAC) by Chinese troops—that too in Eastern Ladakh—in this year itself, have yet again exposed the government's ineptness in dealing with its two intransigent neighbours. While Pak army has exceeded itself with two heinous violations of the cease-fire by its border action teams (BAT-comprising Pakistan army and terrorists raised and supported by it) of beheading two Indian soldiers and killing five on Indian soil amidst a large number of violations to induct terrorists across the LoC, the intrusions by Chinese troops/constabulary of pitching tents and vandalising Indian equipment, followed by many other incursions amount to a new high in their "perceptions" of the LAC. Not only the LoC and LAC, but even the International Boundary from Akhnoor to Kathua has been violated at Hiranagar and Samba, automatic fire and mortars have been rained on the entire border belt of villages, causing fear and evacuations of thousands of people.

Two highly successful tourist seasons in J&K) with all hotels and houseboats full, had proved to be very frustrating for Pak army, the Inter Services Intelligence (ISI), Pakistani jihadi/terrorist groups raised/supported by Pak army and their flunkies/agents in the Kashmir valley. The much improved state of security in J&K making for successful tourist seasons was largely owing to Indian Army's vigil on the LoC becoming more effective by the barbed wire fencing, surveillance devices installed and active patrolling.

Some progress in talks between New Delhi and the elected civil government of Pakistan had resulted in a boost to trade between India and Pakistan. With major complexes for facilitating trade and road freight movement constructed on both sides of the International Boundary between India and Pakistan at Wagah, near Amritsar, Punjab and Chakan Da Bagh, on the LoC had begun functioning. The spurt of visits by Pakistani business delegations to New Delhi and even Mumbai, where in October 2011, they were accommodated in the same Taj Mahal Hotel targeted by Pakistani Lashkar-e-Taiyyaba terrorists during their 26/11 attack. Pakistani traders came to New Delhi in May 2012 to fill up one of the pavilions of Pragati Maidan to showcase their popular products for attracting Indian traders and public. And all this trade dialogue was filled with much talk about Pakistan conferring 'most favoured nation' status. Writing about all these activities in a number of articles, I also kept mentioning how trade was continuing along with cease fire violations along the LoC and terrorist attacks in Kashmir Valley. In my last book titled 'After Abbottabad: Terror to Turmoil in Pakistan', released in November 2012, I brought out how Pak army and jihadis were upping the ante in anticipation of the drawdown of US/coalition forces in 2014 and their plans to substantially step up terrorism against India thereafter.

Intercepts of radio transmissions between Pakistani jihadis, their directors/handlers and their supporters in the Valley in 2012 expressing the frustration at the progress of peace in the Valley and urgent instructions for resumption/increase in momentum of terrorist attacks and spark off tension between security forces and the public, create communal situations leading to violence/bloodshed and incidents which indicated a renewal of attempts to violate the cease fire along the LoC to facilitate entry of Pakistani terrorists into J&K to flare it up again.

In the first half of 2013 itself, the pattern and statistics of Pak an soil/violations by automatic fire and mortar bombardment have been added to these figures. While on 26 September 2013, terrorists highly trained by Pak army or possibly Pak army special forces personnel themselves crossed the International Boundary and attacked a police post in Hiranagar and 16th Cavalry tank regiment in Samba, in two weeks of October alone there were at least 100 violations across International Boundary by automatics fire and mortar bombardment. Army-supported terrorist attacks and ceasefire violations in J&K has been: 20 in January, 24 in February, 29 in March, 28 in April, 27 in May-with 11 incidents on May 24 and 20 incidents in June. Between July and October 2013, almost another 200 attacks were made by entering India.

The total numbers of terrorists killed in 2011 were 95, in 2012 there were 73 and in 2013 the total was 108. While these are figures of terrorists killed, there were an unspecified number who succeeded in infiltrating and launching attacks.

The major differences compared to earlier years are: Pak army's direct involvement with terrorist groups sponsored supported by it; not only participation but Pak army's BATs including terrorists and crossing the LoC to jointly engage Indian troops; while what began in 2012 was spread over the old/former terrorist strongholds like Kupwara, Sopore, Anantnag, Pulwama etc., in 2013, Srinagar got added to the list; the attacks being launched against state police and paramilitary forces—particularly CRPF and BSF—are more daring/innovative and the network of cross-LoC directors /handlers and Kashmiri separatists/agents has been strengthened. Many attempts have been made to create communal/anti security forces disturbances and to step up the frequency of attacks both on the LoC and other parts of the Valley. These are sure indicators of renewed moral, material and monetary support by Pak army for renewing violent terrorist attacks in J&K and also to other parts of India. All these new trends and actions are part of a pattern which began in 2012 and aimed at stepping up even further after American/coalition forces leave Afghanistan in 2014. Indian restraint is emboldening Pak's military-mullah combo all the more.

On 20 May 2013, when J&K Chief Minister Omar Abdullah interacted with the media at the Foreign Correspondents Club of South Asia, New Delhi, I pointed out this pattern of renewal of Pak-sponsored terrorism in J&K since 2012 after two very successful tourist-filled summers and also as a build-up in preparation of 2014, when US would exit from Afghanistan. I also mentioned that Hafiz Saeed had issued a threat of stepping up terrorism in the Valley and that threats and attacks on sarpanches had been stepped up. Mr. Abdullah outrightly denied my contention on both counts. He dismissed what I referred to as a build-up of cross-LoC incidents as "seasonal" and said attacks on *sarpanches* were nothing new or worrisome

Throughout 2012 and till August 2013, New Delhi remaining highly committed to the so-called peace process and talks showing great resolve not to get affected by even the barbaric beheading of two Indian soldiers by Pak army's BAT, umpteen attacks on Indian army/security forces and Kashmiri public and again in August a BAT killing five Indian soldiers, on both occasions entering Indian territory, absolutely beats imagination. And then the statements issued by Indian political leaders vis-a-vis some denials and lies by Pakistani leaders/officials are nothing short of annoying and frustrating to those guarding India's borders, the fraternity of retired servicemen and also the public at large.

Defence Minister A K Antony's initial statement that the attackers were terrorists dressed in Pak army uniforms, contradicting an already issued statement by the Army and the defence ministry that this attack was by Pak army personnel with terrorists came under much criticism by public as well as the opposition.

Reportedly, Pakistani high commissioner Salman Bashir's reaction to the August 6 killing of five Indian soldiers may have been based on an "afterthought". Bashir claimed the Indian DGMO did not raise the killings with his Pakistani counterpart in a hotline conversation hours after the incident.

Indian Army reportedly said the August 6 scheduled talks were at the staff level, and the DGMO himself did not speak to his counterpart. "By the time we had the specifics of the attack, the DGMO sought, by the same evening, an unscheduled call for 10 am the next day. At that call, the DGMO strongly took up the matter," a senior Army officer reportedly said "There was no afterthought at all," he added.

"On the morning of August 6, there was a hotline conversation between DGMO of the two sides and I am told that the Indian side did not mention any violation of the LoC at that time," Bashir said in a TV interview. "So, it seems to me that a lot of constructions are being put on the incident. As I have said, I am not able to put specifics of it," he added. Bashir suggested that India's second official reaction in which it blamed the Pakistan army may have been an afterthought. He was asked if he really thought that India did not initially believe that the attack was carried out by Pakistan army regulars. "I would not say that this is the conclusion I am drawing but it is very evident from the way things have happened in terms of the statements, that there is what I say an afterthought that is involved," he said.

There has been no acknowledgement from Pakistan about any exchange of fire on the LoC which could have resulted in the incident. Pakistani PM Nawaz Sharif, though, in a statement expressed sadness over what he described as loss of precious human lives, it is quite obvious that he is not and may not in the future calling the shots in Pakistan. Sharif also said that he was looking forward to his meeting with Singh in New York in September as he wanted to build trust with India. He said it was incumbent upon the leadership of both sides not to allow the situation to drift and to take steps to improve the atmosphere by engaging constructively with a view to building trust and confidence.

Meanwhile, in an interview to the same TV channel, external affairs minister Salman Khurshid said Pakistan's civilian government must accept responsibility for the attack. "The responsibility must rest with the government. Our meeting point is the civilian elected government of Pakistan, not the Pakistan army or any other agency," he said. Referring to Sharif's statement on killing of five Indian soldiers, Khurshid rued that there was no indication of acceptance of responsibility for the attack even if there was regret. "Whether I can expect or not, we have said that we expect responsibility. That hasn't happened, one. Two, the other concern of what we have been expecting...culpability for what happened in Mumbai. There is no indication of that. And, finally, the statement doesn't take into account, the outreach and the extra mile that India has periodically gone to overcome great difficulties posed," Khurshid said.

On 8 August 2013, after much criticism, Mr. Antony issued a statement which read: "The brutal and unprovoked attack on an Indian patrol on our side of Line of Control (LC) on August 6, 2013 outraged us all. When I reported the incident to the House, it was Government's obligation to report the facts as we knew them at that point of time, and my statement was based on the available information. Since then the Chief of the Army Staff has visited the area and gone into the details of the matter. It is now clear that the specialist troops of Pakistan Army were involved in this attack when a group from the Pakistan Occupied Kashmir (PoK) side crossed the LC and killed our brave jawans. We all know that nothing happens from Pakistan side of the Line of Control without support, assistance, facilitation and often, direct involvement of the Pakistan Army. Those in Pakistan who are responsible for this tragedy and the brutal killing of two soldiers earlier this year should not go unpunished. Pakistan should also show determined action to dismantle the terrorist networks, organisations and infrastructure and show tangible movement on bringing those responsible for the Mumbai terrorist attack in November 2008 to justice quickly. Naturally, this incident will have consequences on our behaviour on the Line of Control and for our relations with Pakistan. Our restraint should not be taken for granted; nor should the capacity of our Armed Forces and resolve of the Government to uphold the sanctity of the LC ever be doubted."

On 9 August 2013, after the Eid festival, there were clashes reported in Kishtwar. The trouble in Kishtwar started as a bike rider was trying to make his way through a procession of Muslims going for Eid prayers. The bike rider reportedly entered into a heated argument with members of the procession. Anti-India slogans were raised led to clashes between the two sides. These clashes resulted in 2 people dead and 20 more injured.

Lt Gen Raj Kadyan, former deputy chief of Army, with whom I interacted, reiterated what he wrote in a recent article in Indian Defence Review: "In just three weeks the Kishtwar riots have entered the penumbra of media attention. Before they fade from memory certain points need to be made. These riots are a vivid reminder of expulsion of nearly four lac Pandits from the Valley. Resemblance is uncanny. The same Hurriyat leaders who had engineered the expulsion of Pandits from the Valley have been behind inciting the Kishtwar riots.... There were two prominent players involved in cleansing out Pandits from the Kashmir Valley. Syed Ali Shah Geelani was the Amir of Jamait-e-Islami which controlled the network of mosques in Srinagar. It was these mosques that broadcast the message 24 hours a day to terrorize the Pandits. The message as translated from Kashmiri was: "We do not want Pandits in Kashmir. We just want their women". Its ominous import was unmistakable. Little wonder that Pandit families with young women were the first ones to run away. The other leader was Muhammad Yasin Malik who led his then underground group JKLF in carrying out selective target killing of prominent Pandits. This added to the terrorisation and accelerated the exodus. The Hurriyat has cleverly kept a few Hindus and Sikhs for window dressing to give their 'freedom struggle' a façade of secularism. These minorities are intended to be kept safe only till the 'freedom' is attained and then they along with the Shia Muslims will meet the same fate as the Pandits. Kashmir Valley is envisaged to become a 100 per cent Sunni fundamentalist State, another North Waziristan, whenever it suits Pakistan or its acolyte, the Hurriyat leaders."

During interaction with this writer, former Army Chief and Member of Parliament, General Shankar Roychowdhury reiterated what he wrote in a leading daily: "Restraint under all provocations seems to constitute the Indian government's core Pakistan policy. Prime Minister Manmohan Singh seems to have detached himself from any public pronouncements and devolved complete authority to the external affairs minister Salman Khurshid. Mr Khurshid is seen at his happiest when riding his pet hobby horse of peace at any cost with Pakistan. Undoubtedly, peace is an important objective as long as it is kept in mind that plausible denial of provocation is a standard response of the Pakistan Army. Pakistan's denial was seen most recently in respect of the revelations made in custody by both Indian Mujahideen co-founder Yasin Bhatkal and an expert bomb maker of Lashkar-e-Tayyaba Abdul Karim Tunda. Given that India has consciously ruled out any option of retaliation in kind, the question is: Are there now any limits on the extent of forbearance by India in respect of habitual prevarication by Pakistan?"

Professional armies are trained to retaliate immediately to any enemy fire or attack, an instinct which has enabled a large percentage of Indian public to enjoy reasonably secure environment, unlike those residing near/on India's borders with Pakistan and China, who suffer much more when the responses to such attacks are not commensurate. There are many instances of Indian Army battalions on the LoC responding promptly and appropriately to violations/unprovoked fire or attacks on their posts, but for the violations mentioned, or since 26/11 and others and particularly in 2013 at least, there is a strong perception by many watchers that government is bending backwards by not wanting/very subtly restraining to approve or actually preventing basic border management pertaining to India-Pak/Sino-Indian context. Not only the LoC and LAC, but even the International Boundary from Akhnoor to Kathua has been violated. Beginning from attacks by Pakistani terrorists highly trained by Pak army/possibly Pak army special forces personnel at Hiranagar and Samba on 26 September, in October, automatic fire and mortars have been rained repeatedly on at least 50 BSF border outposts and on the entire border belt of villages, causing fear and evacuations of thousands of people. These attacks by Pak rangers across the International Boundary may not have been repeated and so extensively, had the retaliatory response been timely and appropriate.

Since the 1993 bombings in Mumbai (just before which the relationship between ISI and Dawood Ibrahim/his Mumbai underworld underlings got cemented), attack on Parliament, 26/11 terrorist attack by ISI, LeT, al-Qaeda etc. or the 2013 attacks by intrusion across the LoC and the very recent ones across the International Boundary—all went un-retaliated, or at least, not appropriately enough. Indira Gandhi, at least till 1971, had her national security instincts in place. Her response to the Chinese upping the ante in Nathu La, Sikkim in 1967 overturned her father's disastrous policy on China and who in 1971 did everything right till the Simla talks, when she fell for Zulfikar Bhutto's dramatics and lies. Pakistan will very well understand the language of without fail retaliation of any military or terrorist attack and also if the Indian government exercising the option of developing the capability to strike at terrorist leaders who motivate the masses at Muridke, Karachi, Lahore or anywhere else in Pakistan. Such retaliation requires not only Indian Army's quick and unrestrained responses on the LoC or the International Boundary, but also for the Indian government to exercise the political will to launch covert targeting into Pakistan to strike at terrorist leaders and camps. India's response to the Kargil intrusion was about six months late as Pakistan army had raised 12 battalions of Northern Light Infantry which had begun crossing the LoC in late 1998 itself, when Musharraf was still the DG, Military Operations. Forget about a leader or a government responding like in 1967 and 1971, today we are caught in a web of vote-bank/twisted secularism politics, in which our key leaders are vying to score self-goals on national security and refusing to orient their instincts or straightening their spines to maintain this independence after ten centuries of being marauded, converted by the sword and ruled. All we can do, it seems so far, is to hope and pray that on the principle of no matter how long the night there has to be a dawn, wait and watch as we lose more trained soldiers and innocent citizens alike.

Chinese very well understood the kind of message sent by the fierce Indian retaliation in Nathu La, in 1967. When People's Liberation Army (PLA) upped the ante there with repeated instances of small arms and heavy mortars, killing some Indian officers and soldiers, then Prime Minister Mrs Indira Gandhi, holding charge of defence ministry also, sanctioned use of artillery requested for by the Nathu La brigade commander. Indian Army's ensuing action resulted in killing about 400 PLA troops and destroying many bunkers and vehicles. In 1986, a PLA unit marched seven kilometres inside across the LAC at Somdurong Chu, Arunachal Pradesh. Then Army Chief General K Sundarji ordered airlifting troops and surrounding their camp by pitching tents a mere 10 metres away, as artillery guns were positioned on nearby heights. The Chinese withdrew. And while Chinese have not resorted to bullets, bayonets, mortars or missiles/rockets since at Nathu La in 1967, unlike Pakistan, there is no saying when that may change as their incursions have been rising. Even without any firing, Chinese have disturbed peace and tranquillity often enough. Will New Delhi assert itself? If so, when and how?

India's Homeland Security Needs More Momentum

In February 2013, over 4 years after the deadly multi-mode and multi-target attack by Pakistani terrorists in Mumbai, Maharashtra State Chief Secretary Jayant Kumar Banthia, speaking to media at the side lines of commissioning of Indian Coast Guard interceptor boat ICGS C-154, announced that Maharashtra is in the process of raising a full-fledged coastal police force. Banthia said the state is developing 4 small ports mainly for shipping, but which will also have facilities allocated for the Coastal police. He said that the landing points along the shore will also get a coastal police station.

Following the 1999 Kargil war, a recommendation by the Group of Ministers to establish a coastal surveillance chain was taken seriously only after the 26/11 terrorist attack. Out of the 9 coastal states and 4 coastal union territories, Maharashtra, which has had mixed successes in implementing coastal security, now plans to raise an exclusive coastal force instead of one comprising personnel on deputation from the existing police setup. Coast Guard's notification to the state government in 2011 that at least 3000 special officers will be required to guard 720 km of Maharashtra's coastline has finally been implemented.

Over two months after 26/11, the Technical Seminar on Internal Security, organised by the Confederation of Indian Industry (CII), with a major participation by Association of Police & Security Suppliers (APSS) the sister trade association of the Defence Manufacturers Association (DMA), United Kingdom held on 4 and 5 February 2009 in Delhi, reflected how ill-equipped Indian internal security agencies were in effective modern gadgetry. During that Seminar, Shaun Hipgrave of UK's Forensic Telecommunications, interacting with this writer expressed, "huge education in the field of telephone forensic measures was a major requirement in India", where prior to 26/11, there was neither much knowledge nor consciousness about such equipment. In fact, shortly before the Mumbai attack, Hipgrave had met the late former head of Maharashtra Anti-Terrorist Squad, Mr Hemant Karkare, who was exploring the market for urgent requirements.

Out of the 46 radar stations based on lighthouses (36 on main land and 10 in islands) located on the East Coast, West Coast, Lakshadweep and Minicoy (L&M) and Andaman and Nicobar (A&N) Islands, the progress is that barring 6 lighthouses in the L&M region where work is in progress, 40 have been fitted with radars. Each lighthouse site will be linked to the nearest Coast Guard station, known as Remote Operating Stations (ROS), through a communication link. The ROS will further be linked to the Regional Operating Centres (ROC) at

Coast Guard Regional headquarters located in Mumbai, Gandhinagar, Chennai and Port Blair. All ROCs will be connected to Control Centre (CC) headquarters at New Delhi.

According to a white paper released at INDISEC 2010 jointly by ASSOCHAM and KPMG strengthening homeland security in India would entail the following steps, some of which have already been initiated by the Government of India:

- Encouraging greater public-private participation, allowing access to and adoption of latest technologies and leveraging the growing defence sector-specific competencies created within the country;
- Further strengthening of the police and paramilitary forces and intelligence machinery at the Centre and in the States through better manpower, training, equipment and other related support;
- Support greater private-public-partnerships and platforms for interactions between the Government and Corporate Institutions, creating a cohesive ecosystem;
- Defining the minimum standards for contracts, equipments and training clearly to enable transparency in overall procurements;
- Holistic expansion of defence offset policy under the Defence Procurement Procedure (DPP) to include equipment for the Homeland Security sector;
- Enhanced critical infrastructure protection through increased physical security and better access control systems at vital installations by leveraging the latest technology;
- Full and effective utilisation of funds under the Police Modernisation Scheme, Coastal Security Scheme, Backward Districts Initiative and other developmental schemes;
- Improve the overall governance and delivery systems of public goods and services; and
- Citizen involvement initiatives aimed at encouraging citizens to partner in safeguarding the internal security environment of the country.

While much more needs to be done to achieve the above, one very crucial requirement for India's security is to develop covert capability to strike at cross-border attackers in their lairs or safe-houses.

Where does the Border Defence Cooperation Agreement with China Place India?

The initial news reports by journalists accompanying Prime Minister Manmohan Singh to China in October 2013 about India "talking tough" or the bonhomie at the banquet hosted by Chinese Premier Li Keqiang with old Hindi films hit songs like 'mera naam chin chin choo' etc, obviously could not be taken too seriously. Because a close look at the Border Defence Cooperation Agreement (BDCA) reveals its sheer ambiguity that ties India into knots. The fact that such an agreement got signed by India only further confirmed the Indian government's utter spinelessness in dealing with the Chinese.

Analyses by a cross section of China watchers bring out how brazenly the clauses in the articles of this agreement have been inked by China and how they will further confuse Indian Army/Indo-Tibetan Border Police/any other force's personnel deployed on the 4057 km-LAC. Such confusion for personnel already operating in a very exacting environment of trying to constantly talk/convince belligerent Chinese troops at every incursion of the variedly 'perceived'/disputable LAC, will inevitably lead to loss of morale.

Some comments by experts on China, with whom this writer interacted with are downrightly disturbing.

Lt Gen (retd.) Prakash Katoch: "Li Keqiang's googly dealt to Manmohan Singh, who has, in connivance the Foreign Minister and National Security Advisor, swallowed it hook, line and sinker and shocked even veteran diplomats, is another massive foreign policy failure that history will not forgive this government for."

Mr Jayadeva Ranade, Member, National Security Advisory Board, former Additional Secretary in the Cabinet Secretariat, Government of India, expressing his personal view, feels uneasy about the new feature in Article VI, as does Katoch. He said that the clause, "...the two sides agree that they shall not follow or tail patrols of the other side in areas where there is no common understanding of the LAC in the India-China border areas" will "leave Indian troops very ambiguous about the manner of responding to an intruding patrol." Ranade is also apprehensive about Chinese army distancing itself from the BDCA and on no mention of the Brahmaputra (Yarlung Tsangpo) river in the river management issues. He added that the government-owned think-tank Chinese Academy of Social Sciences recommended that China ignore India's protests and go ahead with the project to divert the river.

Dr Swaran Singh, School for International Studies, Jawaharlal Nehru University, could not help quipping, "It was a good farewell summit to an elderly statesman from emerging young leaders of China—high on personal gestures and low on substances...the Indian PM also played to the tune by emphasizing on futuristic strategic issues of Sino-Indian relations....The economic deficit was not touched at all".

The already existing agreements between India and China are Maintenance of Peace and Tranquillity Along the Line of Actual Control in the India-China Border Areas signed on 7 September 1993; Agreement on Confidence Building Measures in the Military Field Along the LAC in the India-China Border Areas; the Protocol on Modalities for the Implementation of Confidence Building Measures in the Military Field Along the LAC in India-China Border Areas signed on 11 April 2005 and the Agreement on Establishment of a Working Mechanism for Consultation and Coordination on India-China Border Affairs signed on 17 January 2012. All these have been violated not only in the Eastern segment of the LAC—in Sikkim and Arunachal Pradesh—but also repeatedly in the Western segment's Eastern Ladakh since 2010 at least. And that too where Chinese and Pakistani forces are in close proximity and have been exercising together. What then can be the future be for India after it has signed on the dotted line of a BDCA deviously devised by China?

Indian Army's Aims and Budget Cuts

Inputs and updates on various aspects and issues were shared by Army Chief Gen Bikram Singh with media on 13 January and during his address at the Army Day Parade on 15 January 2014.

Beginning with Government's sanction for raising a mountain strike corps, Gen Singh informed that 22 major and minor units had been raised, the flag of the new corps was raised on New Year's day at its temporary headquarters in Ranchi and that special attention was being paid to forming quick reaction forces and infrastructure development along the borders.

On the Armed Forces Special Powers Act (AFSPA) in J&K, he stated: "As per the military's perspective, (in view of) the situation prevailing in the valley, I think we should wait and watch for a while to see whether the situation remains the same, worsens or improves. Based on that we should take action." He added that developments in Afghanistan also needed to be watched this year and cautioned that there may be a certain amount of spill-over from Afghanistan into Jammu and Kashmir. "There are certain inputs alluding to this already. And, therefore, we need to be on guard," he said. Reminding that the AFSPA was a national decision, which the army was implementing, he stressed that Indian army had "zero tolerance" for human rights violations.

A significant statement Gen Singh made with reference to border violations was that the army would not be easily provoked, "Our country wants to move ahead. These (ceasefire violations) are issues at the tactical level and tactical level operations should not impinge on the strategic initiatives of the nation, which are for growth of the nation in a regional context. They are part of the grand strategy of the nation. My job is to ensure that I engage the adversary where necessary to the quantum of force that is required and do not escalate the situation into one that will impinge on the strategic initiatives."

On modernisation/acquisitions the Chief covered many items/issues: Augmentation of artillery firepower, including a 3-year stock of training ammunition; acquiring of night vision devices, upgrading of mechanised forces and also a time-bound plan to enhance the capabilities of the aviation corps. Security consciousness, cyber security and inter-services cooperation are being stressed upon. Stressing on the importance of superior equipment and firepower for the Army, he said a country is respected only when it is economically and militarily powerful.

Dwelling on the Army's efforts to deal with issues ranging from suicides to shortage of officers and facilities for its serving and retired personnel, the Chief said the shortfall of officers will come down to 10 per cent by 2018 from existing 20 per cent. Additional avenues for permanent commission for women officers are being pursued as a focused key result area.

"Unpleasant incidents" like suicides were down by 50 per cent last year, owing to good administration by commanding officers. Expressing concern for the retired community, he said Army units had begun adopting elderly veterans who were lonely and without a shelter and that an old age home would come up in Panchkula by this year end and another would be constructed in Lucknow. Other welfare measures include trying for increased family pension, cheaper home loans and pension for war-widows as well as mentally and physically-challenged children of personnel. The Army would continue to push for 'one rank one pay', he said, adding that there is more equity in pension now.

Ironically, timed with the Army Chief's announcements, came the news about a cut of over Rs. 7,800 crore from the defence budgetary allocation for this year. While in the fiscal year till 31 December, over 82 per cent of the budget has reportedly been spent for modernisation, with all that is pending, it remains to be seen how unkind this cut will be.

Will Myanmar Commander-in-Chiefs Visit Make any Difference?

Myanmar Army's Commander-in-Chief Vice Senior General Soe Win, accompanied by his wife and six staff officers came on a six-day visit to India in the second week of December 2013. Arriving at Kolkata, he met Eastern Army Commander Lt Gen Dalbir Singh. Gen Win and officers of the Eastern Command discussed issues concerning security and enhancement of military ties between the armies and other issues of mutual interest between the two countries. Received in New Delhi by Army Chief General Bikram Singh, the delegation called on President of India Pranab Mukherjee and Defence Minister A K Antony.

"Bilateral relations between India and Myanmar have seen accelerated growth and expansion over the past two years and India stands ready to build on this". Mr. Mukherjee said India has in the last two years sought to extend and broaden defence cooperation with Myanmar, and is willing to expand the scope of bilateral ties particularly at a time when Myanmar is engaged in far-reaching political and economic reforms and expressed confidence that the Vice Senior General's visit would further strengthen the relations between the two countries. Responding to the President, the Vice Senior General said that Myanmar Government was aware of the importance of peace and cooperation on the border and it stands ready to increase its cooperation with India. He reiterated the assurance made jointly by the Prime Minister and Myanmar President in May 2012 that territories of either country would not be allowed to be used for activities inimical to the other, including for training, sanctuary and other operations by terrorist and insurgent organisations and their operatives.

From Delhi the delegation went to Dimapur, Nagaland and Imphal, Manipur and then back to Myanmar. Defence sources reportedly declined to comment on whether border alignment and fencing issues in Manipur were also raised during the meet.

While this visit coming after Army Chief Gen Bikram Singh's five-day visit to Myanmar in October may appear to be of special significance in the light of enhanced defence cooperation between the two countries and the growing relationship, the fact remains that many past promises by Myanmar of not allowing Indian Insurgent Groups (IIGs) sanctuary in Myanmar, were never actually fulfilled on the ground in past years. Myanmar army however has always been trying to get whatever doles of defence equipment possible from India.

On 28 August, Mullappally Ramachandran, Minister of State of Home Affairs, in a written reply to a question in the Lok Sabha, had reportedly stated: "There are reports that IIGs have been using Myanmar territory for safe sanctuary....Manipur based Meiti insurgent groups like People's Liberation Army (PLA), United National Liberation Front (UNLF), People's Revolutionary Party of Kangleipak (PREPAK); Naga insurgent group like National Socialist Council of Nagaland/ Khaplang (NSCN/K) and United Liberation Front of Assam (ULFA) Anti-talk faction and National Democratic Front of Bodoland (NDFB) have their camps/hideouts in Myanmar Naga Hills (MNH)...Myanmar has always been assuring India that they will not allow their soil to be used by IIGs to carry out activities inimical to India. IIGs continue to use Myanmar territory notwithstanding Myanmar's repeated assurances not to allow its territory for activities inimical to India."

The minister said the presence of IIGs in Myanmar has been the single most important security issue for India at every bilateral negotiations, i.e., National Level Meeting (NLM) at Home Secretary Level and Sectoral Level Meeting (SLM) at Joint Secretary Level held every year in pursuance of 1994 Memorandum of Understanding (MoU) between India and Myanmar. In the NLM between India and Myanmar at Nay Pyi Taw (Myanmar) held in January and SLM held at Kolkata in June, the issue of continued presence of IIG groups in Myanmar was raised again and Myanmar had assured to co-operate closely to address the Indian concerns. "As a result of regular National Level and Sectoral Level Meetings and follow-up of deliberations of NLM and SLM, Myanmar authorities have shown willingness to act against these militant groups and have started some operations against IIGs in Myanmar in recent times," the minister had said.

However, there are no reports of any such implementation so far. The terrorist groups mentioned need to be neutralised for any Look East initiatives to succeed.

Government's Casual to Callous Attitude Towards National Security

Upholding moral responsibility following a fire accident on board submarine INS Sindhuratna, about 40 nautical miles off Mumbai, killing two officers and injuring seven sailors, Admiral D K Joshi resigned as the Naval Chief on 26 February 2014.

Nine days later on 7 March 2014, Commander Kuntal Wadhwa, chief engineer-designate, INS Kolkata, was killed when a valve that came loose that drenched him in carbon dioxide. "The valve that came loose to suffocate and kill Kuntal Wadhwa could be a creation of bad design, shoddy workmanship, inadequate quality assurance, unwieldy procurement methods, callous system, inordinate shipbuilding delays, unwise utilisation of funds or even downright corruption. Or it could be a combination of all these", stated Capt. Ramesh Babu, IN (retd.), Wadhwa's former commanding officer. Number of other naval accidents has preceded these two.

On 14 March 2014, Supreme Court agreed to hear a PIL seeking a court-monitored probe into the fire on board INS Sindhuratna and a compensation of Rs. 1 crore each for relatives of the two officers who died. Claiming that the officers died allegedly due to technical and maintenance failure of batteries in the submarine, the petition sought a court-monitored probe to ascertain whether there was a timely provision of batteries and other safety equipment and also sought a direction for producing the communication between the Defence Ministry and the Navy relating to the maintenance of submarines, particularly Sindhuratna.

Former Naval Chief Admiral Sushil Kumar speaking to me stated: "There has always been an uneasy relationship between the armed forces and the defence ministry. The crisis in the Indian Navy brought out two contrasting perspectives. On one hand there is the binding ethos of our armed forces, and on the other is the disconnect between the ministry of defence and the armed forces, which are its constitutional responsibility. Admiral D K Joshi's decision to resign was an imperative of honour. Accepting moral responsibility for the operational mishaps that occurred during his tenure was laudable, but whether he needed to put in his papers is debatable. By accepting the navy chief 's resignation with surprising readiness, defence minister A K Antony appears to have not only distanced himself from the problems that plague the navy but has passed the buck down the line."

Interacting with me, Bharat Verma, Editor, Indian Defence Review stated: "Antony, possibly the longest serving and the most 'honest' defence minister will probably be remembered for the unprecedented number of scams that happened during his tenure and nothing more. For all the professed honesty that Antony touted on taking over, should have made him clean up the rampant existing corruption in defence public sector units and ministry of defence. Under his leadership it appears that the primary national objective is not to add military capabilities to ensure the nation's security but to find ways to guarantee maximum kickbacks....Antony is unable to control the babus in the MoD and the result is unbridled corruption inside the ministry....The Defence Procurement Procedure created by Antony and the babus of the MoD and often claimed by them to have been improved, continues to be a huge obstacle course in procurement, which is difficult to fulfill by foreign vendors."

It is not only the political leadership, which is apathetic to defence preparedness, but bureaucracy too. Forget about sanctioning and expediting acquisitions, there was the great bogey of an attempt at a military coup. "Antony has not ordered a retired Supreme Court judge to investigate the 'fake military coup' that former Defence Secretary Shashi Kant Sharma tried to create, to malign the Indian Army. Responsibilities need to be fixed as to why the MoD was hell bent on demoralising its own army", reminded Bharat Verma.

Military might and firepower levels of all three services are at an all time low. The holdings of India Air Force (IAF) are far from sufficient to tackle the emerging China-Pakistan combo on multiple fronts. A parliamentary panel was informed that IAF is critically deficient of trainer aircraft and simulators; fighter squadrons are depleting and some airfields do not have certain landing facilities. The IAF has 34 fighter squadrons against the sanctioned strength of 42 squadrons and the number is likely to reduce further to 31 during the 12th plan period. Induction of new or upgraded aircraft has not been commensurate with the de-induction. IAF requires 181 Basic Trainer Aircraft (BTA), 85 Intermediate Jet Trainers (IJT) and 106 Advanced Jet Trainers (AJT). It does not have a Basic Trainer Aircraft as HPT-32 fleet has been grounded after a fatal accident on 31 July 2009.

The submarine fleet of the Indian Navy is at an alarmingly low tally which not only gravely affects its underwater warfare capability, but is also taking a toll of officers and sailors lives in peacetime. Over the past 8 years or so the Navy's operational commitments have substantially increased owing to terrorism and piracy on high seas and more so after the 26/11 Pakistani terrorist attack on Mumbai. With the extent and categories of threats India faces, an effective full-strength submarine arm is of vital importance.

For the Army there has been no purchase of artillery guns for 27 years lies empty, since the Bofors scam. Anti-aircraft guns are ancient. 333 infantry battalions have not been modernised and seriously lack mobility and sufficient firepower. Defects found in 5.56 INSAS rifles necessitate their replacement.

Following former Army Chief Gen V K Singh's letter to the Prime Minister on critical deficiencies in equipment much concern was expressed by the parliamentary committee. In its report tabled in Parliament the panel stated: "The committee is alarmed over the way the deficiencies have been allowed to persist leading to criticality in the Army aviation and ammunition in the country.... The issue of critical gaps should be addressed without any further delay". The report said acquisitions should be put on the fast-track mode. "There are huge gaps between the sanctioned and the existing machines with Army aviation. If the sanctioned and the existing strength is compared, there is shortage of 18 Cheetah, 76 advanced light helicopter (ALH) and 60 ALH with weapons system integrated (WSI). Tank ammunition is another critical area having shortages...Another area affecting the Army preparedness is requirement of guns for our Army.... The upgradation of the Bofors guns is taking a long time. The committee disapproves of the way the deficiency of gun systems has been allowed to reach to the criticality," the report noted. It also stated how blacklisting of certain companies like the Rhinemetals Air defence and Israel Military Industries had hit the acquisition of air defence guns and tank ammunition. The report says, "The committee deplores the way the ministry has dealt with the issue of weight of Bullet-proof Jackets (BPJs) whereby it has been stated that the soldier is not required to wear the BPJs at its maximum weight under low threat levels."

An excerpt of Lt Gen Vijay Oberoi, former Vice Chief from his article The security imperatives for the next PM in *The Tribune*, Chandigarh, 31 March 2014 is relevant.

The much vaunted procurement organisation of the Ministry of Defence (MoD), which has incidentally been reorganised at least six times in the last 15 years or so, has produced zilch. It is unable to expend even the meagre allocated capital budget. It is not that the armed forces do not plan adequately, but it is lack of commitment and understanding of matters military by the MoD, redundant procedures and sitting on files to make money on the side that are responsible for cases not fructifying.

The army seems to have suffered most as far as modernisation is concerned, as its budgetary allocations have decreased considerably. The equipment state of the two fighting arms—armour and infantry—is abysmal. On paper, India fields a total of 3,274 tanks. Of these, only 485 T-90s and 124 Arjuns can be considered modern and even these have major problems like inadequate night fighting capability and sufficient ammunition and spares support. The equipment state of the mechanised infantry is similar. Tracked vehicles, which should have been replaced decades back, continue to be on the inventory of units.

The infantry, which is the mainstay of the army, continues to be equipped with obsolete INSAS rifles. The much vaunted project of fielding state of the art modern infantrymen under the Futuristic Infantry Soldier as a System (F-INSAS) programme is way behind schedule. The infantry is also short of a large number of carbines, machine guns, anti-material rifles, mine-protected vehicles, night-vision devices, bullet-proof jackets and other equipment. Our special and airborne forces are still not equipped with appropriate weapons and combat systems.

The sad saga of equipping the artillery with modern guns is too well known to bear repetition. The equipment state of the Air Defence Artillery is even worse, as they continue to field obsolete weapons of 1970's vintage. The Army Aviation Corps (AAC) continues to fly obsolete Chetak and Cheetah helicopters. For nearly a decade, there is only talk of procuring approximately 200 light utility helicopters, as contracts keep getting delayed or terminated.

The navy is also badly off. The state of naval platforms, both surface and sub-surface is too well known in recent months to need any elaboration. The submarine arm is particularly badly off. A brilliant Chief of Navy Staff has had to resign owning moral responsibility because he has character, although it is not he who should have resigned but the Minister of Defence and the bureaucrats who could not provide equipment and spares, despite being constantly reminded of the bad equipment state.

The state of the air force is equally precarious. It is desperate for more fighters. Its 34 squadrons will reduce to 26 in 2017, if the Medium Multi-Role Combat Aircraft, Rafael, is not inducted by then. There is urgency to replace the ageing MiG fighters, 482 of which have crashed in the last four decades. Their replacement, the indigenous Tejas fighters, continue to be on the assembly line, but none have been produced as yet.

Joint endeavours remain frozen although everyone talks about them. A so-called Integrated Headquarters is in existence as a result of the recommendations of the Group of Ministers (GoM) of 2001, but it is headless as no Chief of Defence Staff (CDS) or Chairman Joint Chiefs of Staff has been appointed. The main reason is that the bureaucracy only believes in retaining and expanding its turf and powers and is least concerned with the security of the nation. The Department of Ex-servicemen Welfare is a joke, as it is more concerned with taking hapless veterans to courts instead of assisting them. The political leadership has long been blasé about the armed forces and prefers not to deal directly with the military hierarchy. Vintage structures continue and forming integrated theatre commands are only talking points in seminars.

We have been unable to formulate a national security strategy as the political leadership has sacrificed merit and has placed its reliance only on loyalists and yes-men in the office of the National Security Adviser (NSA) and in other key positions, instead of people who understand grand strategy and military strategy. Since the inception of the office of NSA, we have had only diplomats and police officers heading it. Consequently, we depend exclusively on "soft power" and enacting more laws, but see no merit in pursuing "hard power."

Despite a lot of lip service, we have not taken any serious actions to indigenise defence production. We continue to waste precious funds on inefficient and corrupt organisations like the Ordnance Factories, Defence PSUs and the DRDO, where middlemen rule the roost. We have ignored private companies which are efficient, have the expertise and are keen to produce defence equipment.

One can continue in this vein and list out all structural and equipment weaknesses, but with no transformation, utter lack of any modernisation of weaponry, and existing shortages of all types of equipment and munitions, the Indian military is not in a position to fight and win battles and wars. We seem to have psyched ourselves to believe that our country will not be embroiled in any war, forgetting that our growth as a military power is an essential component of our ascendancy to "great power" status. No amount of economic development can be sustained unless it is underpinned by military security of a very high order.

The new Prime Minister must initiate urgent measures, to seriously overhaul the present defence machinery, modernise it and make it responsive to the needs of the Indian military and the nation.

Urgent measures to be taken include the integration of Service Headquarters and MoD, simplification of financial vetting procedures, delegation of powers for capital procurements, increasing the processing capacity of the procurement authorities, proceeding rapidly towards joint endeavours, placing professional experts in important positions, setting in motion the comprehensive restructuring of ordnance factories, defence PSUs and DRDO, opening defence production to the trade and above all, having a continuing dialogue with the armed forces hierarchy instead of continuing with the present archaic and peculiar system of interacting with them through middlemen like bureaucrats, diplomats and other civil officials. The Indian military has proven its credentials of loyalty, apolitical demeanour and love for the country and needs to be trusted unequivocally.

Cross-border terrorism by Pakistan not only continues, with unprecedented kind of attacks in 2013, but is expected to increase with the drawdown of US coalition forces from Afghanistan this year. That only raises the possibility of another war. Are those responsible for depriving the armed forces waiting for yet another war to react?

Admiral D K Joshi's resignation and the Henderson-Brook's report on the 1962 Chinese Aggression, a part of which was recently leaked out by Australian writer Neville Maxwell, only further prove that the government has not learnt from past mistakes. It is only by learning from history that a country can manage its geography.

National Security-Related Issues from Bharatiya Janata Party's Election Manifesto 2009

BJP's robust commitment to securing the nation against its enemies is well known. Our first priority will be to take stern steps against terrorists, cross-border or home-grown. An improved POTA-type law will be introduced. The intelligence mechanism shall be overhauled. India's 4000-km long coastline will be fully protected by enhanced naval security.

We will systematically detect, detain and deport illegal immigrants who have emerged as a major source of homegrown terror. Fencing of the India-Bangladesh border, deliberately neglected by the UPA in pursuit of vote bank politics, will be speedily completed.

Use coercive diplomacy to isolate and compel countries engaging in exporting terror across the border to stop their misadventure.

Ensure that the foreign tap of separatist groups in India is completely turned off.

Wage a relentless war against Maoist groups throughout the country using the highly successful and popular Chhattisgarh model.

Introduce a comprehensive National Identity Card for all citizens of India.

Jai Jawan in Action

- All members of the armed forces and the para-military shall be exempted from payment of Income Tax. This will benefit nearly 20 lakh people.
- Take steps to set up a separate Pay Commission for the armed forces. Also revisit the existing pay structure to ensure a better deal.
- Implement one-rank-one-pension.
- Push State Governments to introduce better schemes for the rehabilitation of ex-servicemen and explore avenues for resettling them with gainful employment.

Extracts from BJP's April 2014 Manifesto on Internal Security

BJP will:

- Revive the anti-terror mechanism that has been dismantled by the Congress, strengthen the role of NIA and put a system in place for swift and fair trial of terror related cases.
- Reform the National Security Council to make it the hub of all sector-related assessments. It will be accountable for real-time intelligence dissemination. Digital and Cyber security will be a thrust area.
- Insulate intelligence agencies from political intervention and interference.
- Completely revamp the intelligence gathering system by modernising the intelligence department.
- Provide the State governments with all assistance to modernise their respective police forces and equip them with the latest technology. This will be taken up on a mission mode approach.
- Strengthen and expand the Civil Defence and Home Guards mechanism to create a group of citizens for community defence, self-defence and disaster management.
- Encourage and strengthen NCC training at the college and University level.
- Chalk a national plan in consultation and participation of the state Governments, to address the challenges posed by the

Maoist's insurgency. Talks with the insurgent groups will be conditional and within the framework of the constitution.

- Take urgent steps for the safety of the migrant workers and communities from the Northeast and other states.

Extracts from Manifesto of BJP on ***External Security***

BJP will:

- Address the issue of reforms with regards to defence equipment, support services, organisational regards to defence equipment, support services, organisational reforms and other related matters.
- Address the increasing shortage of commissioned and non-commissioned staff in the defence forces on a priority basis, in a time bound manner. Implement one rank, one pension.
- Build a War Memorial to recognise and honour the gallantry of our soldiers.
- Take measures to make Short Service Commission more attractive.
- Set up the National Maritime Authority which will be equipped with the best of infrastructure, and will focus on coastal security.
- Modernise armed forces, and increase the R&D in defence, with a goal of developing indigenous defence technologies and fast tracking of defence purchases.
- Deal with cross border terrorism with a firm hand.
- Review and improve the border management. Punitive measures will be introduced to check illegal immigration.
- Set up four dedicated defence universities to meet the shortage of manpower.
- Appoint a Veterans Commission to address the grievances of veterans, including reforming ECHS and re-employment of ex-servicemen.
- Ensure greater participation of Armed Forces in the decision-making process of the Ministry of Defence.
- Implement measures to improve the efficiency of Armed Forces Tribunals, and minimise appeals by the Government.

- Ensure that servicemen can register and vote from their place of posting. Initiate the process of digitisation of defence land in cantonment and in other places.

Defence Production

- With its skilled human resources and technical talent, India can emerge as a global platform for defence hardware manufacture and software production. BJP will strengthen the Defence Research and Development Organisation (DRDO); encourage private sector participation and investment, including FDI in selected defence industries.
- Technology transfer in defence manufacturing will be encouraged to the maximum.
- We will find solutions to the problems hampering the growth of the defence sector.
- We will encourage domestic industry to have a larger share in design and production of military hardware and platforms for both domestic use and exports, in a competitive environment.

Devious Designs to Disintegrate India

Breaking India: Western Interventions in Dravidian and Dalit Faultlines, by Rajiv Malhotra and Aravindan Neelakandan, is an important and timely book going into the sinister process of undermining India's integrity by three global networks that have well-established operating bases inside India: (i) Islamic radicalism linked with Pakistan, (ii) Maoists and Marxist radicals supported by China via intermediaries such as Nepal, and (iii) Dravidian and Dalit identity separatism being fostered by the West in the name of human rights. This book focuses on the third: the role of U.S. and European churches, academics, think-tanks, foundations, government and human rights groups in fostering separation of the identities of Dravidian and Dalit communities from the rest of India. The book is the result of five years of research and uses information obtained in the West about foreign funding of these India-based activities. The research tracked the money trails that start out claiming to be for "education," "human rights," "empowerment training," and "leadership training," but end up in programmes designed to produce angry youths who feel disenfranchised from Indian identity. The book reveals how outdated racial theories continue to provide academic frameworks and fuel the rhetoric that can trigger civil wars and genocides in developing countries. The Dravidian movement's 200-year history has such origins. Its latest manifestation is the "Dravidian Christianity" movement that fabricates a political and cultural history to exploit old fault lines. The book explicitly names individuals and institutions, including prominent Western ones and their Indian affiliates. Its goal is to spark an honest debate on the extent to which human rights and other "empowerment" projects are cover-ups for these nefarious activities.

Conclusion

I have tried to put across India's various problems, issues, omissions and commissions of governments of the day as well as my own observations and suggestions on matters related to mostly India's external security and some on internal security too. Unfortunately, the report card of over six decades of India's security, barring the phase including the 1967 confrontation with Chinese at Nathu La and 1971 Indo-Pak war/liberation of Bangladesh under Indira Gandhi, reflects poor, shoddy, flawed to disastrous performance/governance.

While Mr. Narendra Modi has been very vocal in expressing his views on some of the issues mentioned in this chapter, there is no doubt that any leader taking up the reigns of the prime minister of this country today will face many daunting challenges in dealing with internal and external security. A huge factor, very detrimental to both internal and external security, is politics mired in twisting and exploiting religion, exploiting caste for vote-banks and unbridled corruption. Reforming and improving many systems in India will be a very long haul. It is far too much overdue, but a beginning must be made.

Some steps which must be taken as soon as possible after the new government settles down are:

1. India must develop the capacity for covert operations well beyond its borders. With the kind of multiple threats it faces

and the many attacks or acts of war that have been launched against it, effective covert strike capability with necessary resources and political will are an absolute must.

2. The military component in diplomacy has always been quite underplayed in India. In all diplomatic missions there should be a military component. In some important countries the Indian military component should be enhanced.
3. OROP and NFU must be implemented. Implementation of NFU will bring about a great positive change. It will motivate officers to serve despite not bring promoted and not resort to premature retirement.
4. The Armed Forces have a special place in the Constitution. Other organisations or services should not be allowed to compare with the Armed Forces, which have this special place in the Constitution for sound reasons. For example, enough damage has been caused to the Army owing to police and other central armed police forces wearing the same kind of combat dress, badges of rank etc.
5. Department of Ex Servicemen in Ministry of Defence should be headed by a serviceman and not a non-serviceman.

4

A Proposed National Security Agenda for Narendra Modi

Maj Gen GD Bakshi

Backdrop

India is now in the midst of the most critical elections in its post-Independence history. There is a dire need for a strong and decisive government in New Delhi to take the bold decisions for pulling India out of the economic morass that the present dispensation has plunged it into. We have seen the onset of petty politics of populism based on wasting precious government resources to give massive doles and freebies instead of focusing on the long-term sustainability of the state by creation of infrastructure, generation of energy and creation of enough jobs. India's armed forces have been neglected for long and their modernisation process has been virtually sabotaged. India stands at a critical crossroads today and the nature of the next administration will determine to a great extent whether India can exploit its massive youth human resource and become a breakout nation. *However, can India fail to kick-start its faltering economy and fail to generate some 200 million new jobs? We may well face an internal security crisis of unprecedented proportions.* The external environment is equally challenging.

- The steep rise in the military and economic power of China poses the most significant security challenge. The rising qualitative and quantitative differential in air power between India and China is opening serious windows of vulnerability.

- The US withdrawal from Afghanistan will unleash a great deal of turbulence in the Af-Pak region that will have major spinoff effects in terms of terrorist violence in J&K and the rest of India.
- The situation in Nepal and Bangladesh and Maldives is passing through a critical phase.
- In the internal security sphere, India today faces serious problems of governance that are destabilising the political economy and delegitimised the current ruling class. This stems from *undue emphasis on short-term political gains through populist measures like unsustainable doles and subsidies. This has halved the GDP growth rate from 9 per cent per annum to just 4.5 per cent per annum; inflation has doubled; the rupee has been devalued by 20 per cent and there is a huge current account deficit.*
- This civilisation challenge has already generated its collective response in terms of a clear realisation in the Indian electorate—especially the middle class, about the need to vote in a strong and stable government. Exit polls clearly indicate a victory for Narendra Modi. The criticality would be the margin of the victory in terms of seats won so that a strong and centralised state emerges in New Delhi that is not dependent on the whims and fancies of the regional satraps. Chances are strong that Modi could emerge with a clear majority on his own.
- What then should be the National Security agenda of the new dispensation in New Delhi? This is briefly summarized in this article.

Military Modernisation Shortfall

The UPA government's misplaced emphasis on doles and subsidies has seriously impacted the defence budget and dangerously slowed down its modernisation process. The pace of arms acquisition has been slowed down to a painful crawl due to arms scandals and a gridlock in decision making.

- Meanwhile the Indian Air force squadron strength has declined dangerously from some 42 squadrons to under 30 squadrons. With the Rafale and LCA nowhere in sight, the scenario is only likely to worsen as old MiG-21s have become outdated and no replacements have been made. What is very dangerous is that for the first time in recent history, the PLAAF has acquired not just a quantitative edge over the IAF but has now also got a clear qualitative edge. China today has some 913 Fourth Generation fighters to just 322 with India. By 2020 the Chinese will have some 1300 Fourth Generation fighters and their Fifth generation aircraft would probably be coming in.
- In the Naval sphere the Chinese have some 55 submarines to India's 11. Even this figure will decline to just 5 when additional Kilos are phased out over the next 2 years and no Scorpenes get inducted due to inexcusable delays in production. The Indian Navy that had Bluewater aspirations, has been reduced by the Ministry to the level of the Pakistani Navy as far as underwater capability is concerned.
- The Army has now been without a Medium gun since the induction of the Bofors in 1987. Medium artillery is a critical factor in mountain warfare and they are needed to protect our borders with the neighbours. India must go in for indigenously produced Medium Guns at the earliest. The entire Air Defence inventory and helicopter fleet of the Army date back to the 1960s. Half of India's tank fleet is still night blind and short of ammunition. All these gaps have opened up huge windows of vulnerability which will be crucial for the next 3-5 years period.

India's Grand Strategic Compulsions

This Military build-up gap has seriously impacted the capabilities of the armed forces to deal with a two-front scenario. The tragic fact is that if we crank in Internal Security, *India faces not just a two-front but a critical three-fronts scenario with China to its North, Pakistan to its west and the Maoist and Jihadis in India's rear. The Central theme of any Indian Grand strategy would be to ensure that we tackle these three fronts consecutively and not concurrently.* Being forced to deal simultaneously with a three-front scenario would be a civil disaster and the primary effort of the Indian state should be to avert such a contingency. This translates into dealing with each front at the time and place of our choice.

The Return of Pacifism and Appeasement Policies

Mindful of the glaring gaps it has opened up in defence preparedness, the UPA administration resorted to a policy of appeasement of all adversaries.

- Not only did it appease the principle security threats from China and Pakistan but it also exhibited a surprising reluctance to use legitimate levels of force against the well-armed Maoist insurgents and Jihadi terrorists sponsored by Pakistan.
- Political expediency has greatly hobbled the campaign against the terrorists. In the struggle against the Maoists, sections of the current ruling party openly hobnobbed with Maoist sympathisers and did their best to sabotage Operation Green Hunt.
- Today, a virtual army of foreign-funded NGOs and Human rights organisations have raised a shrill outcry against all Security Forces operations to deliberately hamper and slow down this campaign. Today the number of people employed in India by the NGOs outnumbers the police forces of India by a wide margin. These NGOs have started a human rights industry that has by design, slowed anti-Maoist operations to a crawl. *The AAP Party is just the latest addition to this NGO phenomenon that is trying to create an "Orange Revolution or Arab Spring" in India and seed chaos and destabilisation. Its primary intention seems to be to ensure that no strong and decisive government comes up in New Delhi.*
- What is painfully visible is the complete lack of political will to tackle external adversaries and internal challengers. The UPA legacy in the National Security domain has generated a stark crisis situation.

Demographic Profile

What lends it criticality is the demographic profile of the Indian population. Today, India has the youngest population in the world. *By 2020 some 68.4 per cent will be in the working age group. Considering that India already has some 145 million unemployed youth, the number of new jobs needed by 2020 would amount to some 483 million.* If we cater solely for the recruitable male population out of this—India still urgently needs to generate some 200 million jobs in the next 5 to 6 years. This is a major challenge. If we can skill our youthful population, India could well emerge as a breakout nation economically. However, a failure to generate adequate levels of employment could create a disaster scenario on the Internal Security front.

Agenda for the New Administration

Economic Reconstruction

The primary task of the new Administration would be to overcome the paralysis in decision making and revive the Indian economy with a focus on long-term sustainability.

- The emphasis will have to shift from short-term doles and subsidies to creation of infrastructure, generation of power and employment on a major scale.
- Tourism generates the highest number of jobs for the capital invested and must be given a major boost.
- The only way to boost employment will be to change our archaic labour laws and encourage the rapid growth of small- and medium-scale industries. Manpower intensive industries like ship building etc. should be our primary focus.
- We must rapidly create a defence industrial base in India's private sector to generate employment and achieve autarky in critical weapon systems.
- The criticality would be to generate at the very least some 200 million jobs by 2020. This would be vital for India's national security.

Speeding up Military Modernisation

While stabilizing the economy, the next administration in New Delhi will have to take concerted steps to speed up the tragically derailed military modernisation process. To start with, the highly undesirable acrimony in civil military relations must be reduced and eliminated. The new dispensation must speedily act upon the recommendations of the Kargil Review Committee and the Naresh Chandra Committee reports. The following would demand operational priority:

- **Air Power**: The most critical gap with China is in the realm of air power. This must be speedily closed with the rapid induction of the Rafale. If that is not possible for any reason, we must quickly acquire more SU-30 Fighters. The LCA and 5th Generation Fighter programmes will have to be accelerated to arrest the alarming decline in the number of fighter squadrons. Air power is critical and India must rapidly build up a strength of 45 squadrons as a bare minimum. Keeping a two-front scenario in mind, India optimally needs a 60-Squadron Air Force with an emphasis on home grown fighters like the LCA and MMRCA.
- **Naval Build-up**: The alarming gaps in our sub-surface fleet must be rapidly plugged by leasing some 4 Kilo/HDW class submarines to tide over the gap created by late induction of Scorpenes. We will have to induct another six Scorpenes or build them at home. We may also have to lease another nuclear submarine. The surface warship building programme must be greatly accelerated.
- **The Army**: The most critical shortfall is in our medium artillery. After the Bofors scandal the Indian Army has not been able to get another medium gun. That may turn out to be a blessing in disguise if Indian firms, either Tata or Kalyani Forge are able to rapidly provide us the 1500 Medium artillery guns that we so urgently need along with their truck/track-based mobile versions. The night blindness of the balance tank fleet must be overcome on operational priority. The Indian infantry needs a new system of small arms urgently and the Air Defence artillery

and Army Aviation helicopter fleet must be rapidly modernised. Critical ammunition inventories must be made up with the greatest of urgency and dispatch. The Ammunition Roadmap must be actualised within the next two years.

- **Infrastructure**: It is indeed astonishing that 50 years after the 1962 war we still have not been able to complete our road infrastructure build up in the Himalayas. This is inexcusable and the border road building programme must be put on a fast track.
- **Nuclear deterrence**: India needs to rapidly operationalise the third leg of its nuclear triad. Considering that the Indian arsenal must deter both China and Pakistan, we will have to increase the number of war heads rapidly to an optimal level that takes care of both adversaries. Media reports that Pakistan alone has more war heads than India are hardly cause for reassurance. India may also need to consider inducting strategic bombers like the Russian Bear/Backfire to add greater flexibility to its triad. Mid-air refuelling of fighter bombers may not be optimal for this task. Bear/Backfire-type bombers with cruise missiles may be an optimal solution.

Internal Security Imperatives

Some 232 of India's 602 districts are affected by the Maoist insurgency. This is virtually one-third of Indian territory. In some 32 districts, the writ of the Indian state has ceased to run.

- These are the mineral rich districts with major deposits of coal, iron, copper and aluminium. *India must rapidly reclaim its own territory* and not leave its development at the mercy of tribal guerrillas. They have effectively deprived the Indian state of its key minerals like coal and aluminium which are now being imported despite being available in large quantity within Indian territory.
- As stated, India is in a three-front scenario with the Maoists and Jihadi terrorists forming the third front. It is vital that India stabilises this internal front as rapidly as possible so that it is

not left as a festering sore to be dealt with at the time of an external crisis.

- *A curious disjunction between the UPA government and the party has not let the Indian state come down hard on the Maoist insurgents.* Operation Green Hunt was launched by Mr P Chidambaram, India's former Home minister. Over 101 CAPF/BSF battalions were deployed along with the state police forces.
- The results have been somewhat mixed. Some notable successes were achieved in eliminating the urban-based Guerrilla leadership cadres and destroying rocket manufacturing factories.
- However, in the densely forested terrain, the guerrillas have simply rolled with the punch. By and large the police operations have just driven them to adjacent areas and adjoining states.
- No appreciable attrition has been inflicted on the hard core PGLA Platoons, Companies and Battalions. In fact, these have repeatedly succeeded in inflicting fairly heavy casualties on the CRPF..

The new administration will have to *decide whether it is more cost effective to raise additional CRPF battalions or raise new army formations that could initially be deployed against the Maoists but would later be available for use against China/Pakistan.* Nowhere in the world has the police been tasked to conduct offensive counter-insurgency operations against well-armed insurgents in such difficult jungle terrain. The CRPF has actually been tasked far beyond its design capabilities.

Crafting an Asian Balance of Power

The period 2014-18 is going to present a window of great vulnerability for Indiabecause of glaring gaps in its military modernisation drive. As such it must seek to redress the highly adverse balance of forces by strong strategic partnerships with countries like Japan and Vietnam which are equally threatened by China.

- In fact, India needs to create a regional balance of power architecture based on the core states of India, Japan and Vietnam and which must also involve South Korea, Philippines, Indonesia and Malaysia—countries that feel threatened by Chinas rising assertiveness.

- Such an alignment of forces would, at the very least, serve to complicate decision making for China and ensure that it is prevented from focusing all its military resources in any one strategic direction and single out any one Asian state for major military aggression.
- Asian balance of power will have to be complimented by an Indian strategic technical partnership with Russia, Israel and France to seek cutting edge military technology and acquire military force multipliers to offset Chinas quantitative advantage.
- The alternative is an alignment/strategic partnership with the USA. This would serve to antagonise China; and the USA, in its current post Iraq/Afghanistan stage, may not be very keen to get embroiled in local wars between China and its neighbours. This could of course, change if relations between the USA and China worsen. As of now, however, the current cost-benefit analysis does not indicate major returns from such a premature alignment with the USA.
- This is complicated by the USAs reluctance to share its cutting edge technology and its inordinate levels of support to Pakistan.

Japan—Key Factor: The relationship with Japan however would be crucial to balancing the economic and military power of China in Asia. Japan has huge investments and has off shored a great deal of its manufacture to China. India could take advantage of the strains in the Sino-Japan relationship to draw this massive Japanese investment to Itself. It can offer cheaper labour and other inducements.

- Japan can give invaluable help in the creation of rail and road infrastructure, power generation and ultimately even in civil nuclear energy.
- *Japan could assist India in creating a defence-industrial base in the private sector and thereby help in developing engines for its jet fighters, warships and tanks.* India would need Japanese help in

cyber war and robotics. It could also assist India in electronic chip manufacture and hardware which are now all being imported at huge cost.

- *However, Japan could make a singular contribution if it would assist India in promoting Buddhist pilgrimage tourism in India on a Haj scale. Not only would this generate millions of jobs but also enhance India's soft power and influence in the whole of Asia.*

5

India's Energy Security: Emerging Challenges

Talmiz Ahmad

Energy security may be defined as the assured access to energy resources at affordable prices to obtain sustainable economic growth rates and national economic development. Given the importance of energy as the foundation of the national and, indeed, the global economy, concerns relating to energy security have deepened in different parts of the world in recent years. This is primarily on account of:

- high global demand and attendant supply constraints, as also geopolitical developments that are continuously creating uncertainties in oil and gas markets and contributing to price volatility; and,
- with supply constraints, there is considerable international competition to secure these resources.

Over the last fifteen years India has emerged as a major consumer of global energy resources. India's present and long-term energy mix is at Table 1.

The following points may be noted in this regard:

(i) in 2035, India will become the third largest energy consuming country in the world after China and the USA, when the Indian share in global energy demand will go up from 4 per cent in 2010 to 8.6 per cent;

Table 1: India's Present and Long-term Energy Mix

Energy source	*2010 (per cent)*	*2035 (per cent)*
Coal	55	52
Oil	31	28
Gas	10	12
Nuclear	-	4
Hydro	-	2
Renewables	-	1
Total energy demand	433 mtoe	1464 mtoe

Source: Yuhji Matsuo, *Asia/World Energy Outlook 2012*, The Institute of Energy Economics Japan (IEEJ), January 2013.

(ii) India's energy demand is expected to increase by 3.8 per cent annually;

(iii) fossil fuels will account for 90 per cent of incremental growth by 2035;

(iv) demand for coal will be driven by the power and industry sectors and will retain its position at over 51 per cent of the national energy mix; these sectors will also propel the demand for national gas;

(v) oil demand will increase from 2.5 mbd in 2010 to 6.9 mbd in 2035; India's import dependence will go up to 87 per cent.

The central challenge relating to India's energy security is that of import dependence. Thus, in regard to oil, while India has 0.7 per cent of world resources, it consumes 3.9 per cent, and is import dependent to the extent of over 80 per cent. Similarly, with regard to natural gas, while India has 0.8 per cent, it consumes 1.9 per cent of world resources. Given these serious domestic shortcomings, the government in the last few years has commissioned two reports to study the country's energy situation and to propose remedial initiatives.

The *Hydrocarbon Vision 2025*, published by the Government of India in February 2000 set out in stark terms India's energy security predicament: its crude oil self-sufficiency had declined from 63 per cent in 1989-90 to 30 per cent in 2000-01; in 2024-25, crude oil self-sufficiency was expected to be a mere 15 per cent. The situation relating to gas was equally grim:from 49 BCM (billion cubic metres) in 2006-07, India's demand for gas was expected to rise to 125 BCM in 2024-25. As against this, production from existing fields and discoveries was 52 BCM, leaving a gap of 75 BCM to be filled through new domestic discoveries and from imports.

This pioneering study was followed by the *Integrated Energy Policy* report, published by the Planning Commission in August 2006 under the Chairmanship of Mr. Kirit Parikh. It took a holistic view of India's energy requirements up to 2031-32. The report postulated that, in order to reach growth rates of 8 per cent per annum up to 2031-32, the country needed to do the following:

- increase primary energy supply three to four times, and,
- expand electricity generation capacity five to six times from the 2003-04 levels, that is, power generation capacity should increase from the current 160,000 MW (megawatt) to nearly 800,000 MW by 2031-32.

The Kirit Parikh report projected several different energy mix scenarios based on the country's achievement in promoting the best use of one or more items in the national energy mix. Four scenarios set out in this report are at Table 2.

Table 2: India's Energy Mix

India's energy mix in different energy use scenarios in 2032 (%)*

	Energy Source	*Energy Mix in 2006*	*Coal Dominant*	*Full use of Hydro, Nuclear & Gas*	*Plus enhanced fuel efficiency*	*Plus maximum use of renewables*
1	Coal	51	54	45.5	42	41
2	Crude Oil	36	26	26	29	23
3	Gas	9	5.5	10.7	10.2	9.8
4	Hydro	2.1	0.7	2	2.1	2.2
5	Nuclear	1.5	4.0	5.3	6	6.4
6	Renewables	0.7	0.1	0.1	0.1	5.6

**Source:* Integrated Energy Policy, Planning Commission, New Delhi, Sep. 2006, p. 44.
Note: In the above figures, non-commercial energy is between 10-12 per cent.

In order to achieve these targets, the report emphasized the importance of the following initiatives to augment domestic resources:

(i) maximising the use of the national hydropower potential,
(ii) obtaining the materials and technology to pursue civilian nuclear power projects,
(iii) pursuing energy efficiency and demand-side management policies, and
(iv) diversifying energy sources through increased use of renewables.

However, in spite of these efforts, the report noted that the following facts would continue to characterize the Indian energy scene:

(i) even if India succeeded in exploiting its full hydropower potential of 150,000 MW, the contribution of hydro energy to the energy mix would only be around 1.9 - 2.2 per cent;
(ii) even if a 20-fold increase took place in India's nuclear power capacity by 2031-32, the contribution of nuclear energy to India's energy mix was also, at best, expected to be 4- 6.4 per cent;
(iii) even with a 40-fold increase in their contribution to primary energy, renewables would account for only 5 to 6 per cent of India's energy mix by 2031-32; and,
(iv) in all scenarios, fossil fuels would be between 74 per cent and 85 per cent of the energy mix, as against 96 per cent at present.

The inevitable conclusion was that, for India's energy security, the country would need to enhance its global engagements through a vigorous energy diplomacy. In order to determine the content and direction of this effort, it would be useful to look at the global scenario which will define the challenges in India's pursuit of its energy security interests.

Global Energy Scenario

Overall, the global energy picture is one of considerable dynamism and even turbulence with regard to both demand and supply. Globally, oil is going through important changes geographically, geologically, chemically and economically. It appears that conventional oil production, while still likely to be a major part of the global energy mix, will increasingly yield space to unconventional oil from a variety of sources, such as: shale oil, oil sands, new heavy oil, deep water oil and production from the Arctic region.[1] Thus, even in the short term up to 2020, global oil supplies could increase by up to 40 million barrels per day due to increased supply of conventional production from Iran and Iraq and unconventional oil from the United States (shale oil), Canada (tar sands) and Brazil (deep water pre-salt). However, in spite of major increases in supply, energy demand from 2010 to 2035 does not show any significant changes in regard to the global energy mix, as brought in Table 3.[2]

Table 3: Energy Demand by Fuel, 2010 and 2035

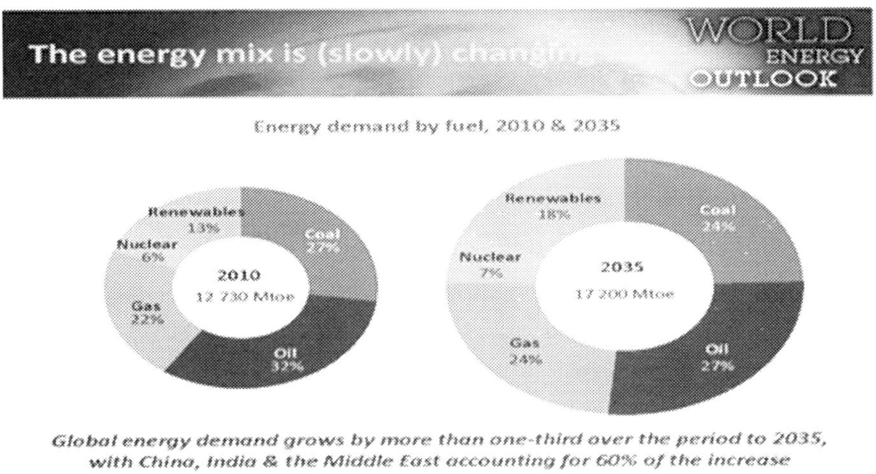

The other aspect of the global energy scenario pertains to the significant increases in Asian demand, a constant feature over the last few decades: between 1970-94, Asian energy demand increased by 400 per cent, with Asia's demand for oil increasing by 265 per cent, while world demand growth during this period was only 63 per cent. The long-term (2035) Asian energy scenario has the following features:

- Asian primary energy demand will go from 4.2 billiontonnes oil equivalent (toe) in 2010 to 7.7 billion toe in 2035;
- In 2035, Asia will account for 40 per cent of global oil demand, going up from 31 per cent in 2010; Asia will also account for 60 per cent of global oil demand growth; and,
- China and India will represent nearly 70 per cent of Asian energy demand in 2035, with China accounting for 52 percent and India 18 per cent; Japan's share will decline from 12 per cent in 2010 to 6 per cent in 2035.

Geopolitics

The global demand-supply situation will be affected by other important factors such as geopolitical developments; climate change concerns; energy efficiency, and the use of nuclear power. The principal source of geopolitical uncertainty pertains to the situation in the Gulf and the West Asia North Africa (WANA) region which provides the bulk of the world's conventional production. Domestic turmoil in Iraq and Libya has created grave concerns relating to the long-term reliability of supplies from these countries, while global sanctions against Iran have restricted the availability of Iranian oil in the world market, a situation that could change quite dramatically once sanctions are lifted.

There are other factors which further complicate the situation. The countries of the Gulf Cooperation Council (GCC),which over the long-term will be the principal suppliers of oil to Asia, will have to invest heavily in their energy sectors so that they are in a position to meet this demand. Already, the major GCC countries have announced significant investments over the next five years: Saudi Arabia ($140 billion); UAE ($76 billion) and Qatar ($41 billion). The sectors benefitting from these investments will be: oil—42 per cent; gas—34 per cent and power—24 per cent.

However, in response to the challenges of the Arab Spring, the GCC countries have also increased their domestic social spending commitments, estimated at about $150 billion over the next five years. This has resulted in the GCC countries requiring a higher oil price threshold to meet both their investment and social spending commitments. Thus, from the GCC perspective, the "fair price" bands have shifted upwards from $22-28 per barrel in 2004, to $40-50 in 2005, and then on to $80 in 2011;it is now hovering between $80-90.

Climate Change

In regard to climate change, the following points may be noted:

- over next 40 years, the world will need twice as much energy with half the carbon emissions;
- many of the concerns posed by current energy trajectories could be eased by shifting more rapidly towards natural gas, unconventional methane deposits and renewable energy systems;
- natural gas is the least environmentally harmful of all hydrocarbons, with a given unit of energy from gas generating about 40 per cent less carbon dioxide than oil, and 75 per cent less than coal; emission from gas of carbon dioxide is one-fifth as from coal; emission of sulphur dioxide and other particulates is negligible; since 2007, the US has cut carbon emissions by 7 per cent and Europe by 10 per cent—half due to shift from coal to gas.
- renewable energy industries (which include hydroelectric, biomass, geothermal, solar, wind, and other modern systems) together provided only around 35 per cent of the commercial energy consumed in 2000.

It is noteworthy that in 2035 non-OECD countries will account for a rising share of emissions, though their per capita share will only be half that of the OECD. On the positive side, there are indications of greater use of renewables in electricity generation globally. In the developing countries, including India and those in Latin America ASEAN and Africa, hydropower will provide the bulk of renewable resources, with other sources being wind and solar. In China, hydropower and wind will be the principal sources, while in the developed countries the main source will be wind.

Nuclear Power

The use of nuclear energy for power generation received a setback after the Fukushima episode in Japan, with an adverse impact on Japan's energy mix in regard to the use of nuclear power in electricity generation. Before Fukushima, Japan had 54 nuclear power units producing 48.96 GWe of power. Since then, 17 units have been shut down (16 GWe), while 35 units (30.70 GWe) are closed due to inspections. Only two are functioning, providing 2.27 GWe of power. The shift to alternative fuels (natural gas and renewables) is already costing the country $123 million per day. New LNG terminals are being set up and Japan is gearing itself to increase its gas imports significantly.

In the rest of Asia, though there are concerns relating to the use of nuclear power, observers suggest that nuclear power could continue to figure prominently in the Asian energy mix for the following reasons:[3]

(i) it provides for energy mix diversification and hence promotes energy security,
(ii) it reduces dependence on imported fuels,
(iii) its operational costs are very low,
(iv) it reduces dependence on supplies from the volatile Gulf region,
(v) it compensates for depleting world fossil fuel reserves, and
(vi) it is environmentally friendly, having no carbon emissions.

Overview

Taking the above factors into account, the following will be the scenario elating to global energy demand in 2035:

(i) global energy demand will increase by one-third from 2011 to 2035;
(ii) emerging economies will account for 90 per cent of net demand growth in 2035, with China, India and the Middle East constituting 65 per cent of the total increase;
(iii) global energy trade will shift eastwards. from the Atlantic to the Asia-Pacific: by the early 2020s, China will become the

world's largest oil importer, while India will emerge as the largest coal importer;

(iv) fossil fuels, which accounted for 82 per cent of energy supply in 2010, will constitute 80 per cent of the global total in 2035; each of the three fossil fuel types (oil, coal and gas) will converge around similar shares of about 26-27 per cent;

(v) long-term oil demand will increase by 20 mbd over 2012-35, reaching 108.5 mbd in 2035; of this increase, developing Asia will account for 88 per cent; and,

(vi) while rising non-OPEC output from North America and Brazil will reduce demand from OPEC suppliers over the next decade, OPEC will regain its role as the key source of oil supply growth from the mid-2020s.

(vii) Saudi Arabia will remain a central player in OPEC and global energy scenarios: it plans to maintain its production capacity at 12.5 mbd, but will develop new fields and extend the life of old fields by lowering their production.

India's Energy Diplomacy

Given India's acute dependence on imports, India requires an energy diplomacy that pursues substantial, robust, multifaceted engagements across the world to promote India's energy security interests. This energy diplomacy will have the following agenda:[4]

(i) enhancement of domestic resources and capabilities;

(ii) acquisition of assets abroad; these are of two types:

  (a) equity participation in producing fields; and,

  (b) exploration and production (E & P) contracts in different parts of the world, both on-shore and offshore;

(iii) participation in downstream projects (refineries and petro-chemicals) on the basis of criss-cross investments;

(iv) pursuit of long-term LNG contracts;

(v) setting up of trans-national gas pipelines wherever feasible; and,

(vi) regional and global producer-consumer dialogue for energy security.

Cooperation for Energy Security

India's energy diplomacy faces serious challenges. About 15 years ago, when China burst upon the global scene with significant increases in its energy demand, certain Western writers were deeply alarmed by this intrusion in an area that had been largely dominated by Western countries and their corporate entities. They had then viewed Chinese energy activism in zero-sum terms, and had even used outdated imperialist rhetoric to describe the new situation, such as: a New Cold War, a New Great Game, and even A New Scramble for Africa. In this fraught environment of competition and confrontation, India has strongly articulated an approach to energy security that is based on regional and global cooperation.[5] The Indian emphasis on cooperation logically flows from certain facts relating to the global energy scene: First, the need to mobilize resources globally:

- hydrocarbon resources to meet global demand over next 30-35 years are available, but new technologies in different countries have to be deployed to yield fresh discoveries and augment supplies from old fields;
- oil is available in physically challenging areas such as the deep sea or frozen terrain or environmentally sensitive locations, which will require a major global cooperative effort to mobilise technology and human resources; and,
- exploration and development of these resources will require rather huge investments, amounting cumulatively to over $ 5 trillion up to 2030, @ $20 billion per annum; these are beyond the capacity of a single corporation or country and will require a major global effort.

Secondly, energy security embraces the protection of the entire energy supply chain and infrastructure: production facilities, transport, refining, pipelines, storage facilities, power plants and transmission lines; for instance:

- currently, daily 40 million barrels of oil cross the oceans in tankers; could come 67 million barrels in 2020; and

- about 150 million tonnes of LNG is transported by sea and could reach 460 MT by 2020. Energy security thus is a transborder effort, requiring the active participation of all stakeholders from the producing field to the end-consumer.

Indian Initiatives

In pursuit of its energy interests, India has built up a series of **bilateral strategic energy partnerships** in order to enhance its domestic capabilities in different areas and obtain access to global resources and technologies to meet its domestic demand.[6] Besides building solid relationships with the principal supplier countries of the Gulf, India has turned to China to cooperate in developing clean coal technologies; to Japan and South Korea to enhance its efficiency capabilities; to Turkey to learn about transnational pipelines, and to Norway to benefit from deep sea exploration technologies.

India also set up platforms for Asian **producer-consumer dialogue,** commencing with two Round Tables in 2005, which laid the foundations for a consensual approach to Asian energy interests. This dialogue has now been institutionalized and takes place every two years at Ministerial level. Again, in a pioneering initiative India commenced dialogue with its neighbours on **transnational gas pipelines**. Though these early negotiations did not result in actual projects due to political constraints, India was able to acquire considerable in-house knowledge of this new sector and will be in a position to revive this dialogue when the political situation in the neighbourhood is more propitious.[7] India is also an active participant in the deliberations of the multilateral energy body, the International Energy Forum (IEF), based in Riyadh.

Gulf-Asia Energy Ties

Asian countries are experiencing a significant change in their status and role in the global economy. Thus, Asian economies continued to show fairly substantial growth in output even after the global financial crisis of 2008-10, with China and India attaining 9.5 per cent and 7.8 per cent growth respectively, while Southeast Asia obtained 5.3per cent.

Though growth rates in Asia have fallen over the last few years as growth in the West has remained sluggish, they are still well above rates in developed countries, with signs of recovery in several Asian countries already apparent.

These trends in favour of Asian economic achievement are expected to continue through the 21st century. By 2025, the Chinese economy will be of the same size as the US economy, with India the fourth largest after Japan; by 2050, the largest economy in the world will be China, which will be twice the size of the US economy, with the Indian economy following a close third, and almost on par with the US. The combined India-China GDP will exceed that of the G-7 OECD economies by 2025; by 2060, it will be more than one and a half times larger. In 2010, India and China accounted for less than half of G-7 GDP, in 2060, the combined GDP of the two will exceed that of the existing OECD area.[8]

Asia's rapid development in the last decade has made the issue of energy security a major challenge for the continent. In Asia's industrialising countries, the average annual energy consumption growth is 3 percent, while this rate is 1.7 percent worldwide. Following the shale revolution in the US and increasing fuel efficiency and use of renewables in the West, there will be sharp declines in dependence on Gulf oil imports in the US and EU. Asia already absorbs about 75 per cent of GCC energy exports: the extent of dependence on the GCC at present is as follows: Japan 70 per cent; ROK 60 per cent; India 50 per cent, and China 30 per cent.

During the next 10-15 years, even as the US reduces its oil imports, most of the Gulf production will shift to Asia: the Asian giants—China, Japan, Korea and India—will depend on Gulf supplies to the extent of 60-90 per cent, while around 90 per cent of Gulf production will go to Asia. The scenario relating to oil exports from the Gulf in 2035 is expected to be as follows:[9]

- China: 6-8 mbd
- India: 5.0 mbd
- Japan and ROK: 4.5 mbd

- Europe: 2.2 mbd
- US: 0.2 mbd

Hence, over the long-term, the security and stability of the Gulf is of crucial importance to the energy-consuming Asian countries. This changing geopolitics of energy has in fact thrown up new opportunities to pursue shared interests that would bring the US, other Western powers and the principal Asian powers in a cooperative security paradigm structured around the GCC countries, Iran and Iraq.[10] The principal Asian energy consumers—China, Japan, Republic of Korea and India —could play a lead catalytic role in pursuing and realizing this new consensual arrangement.

The challenges in realizing this strategic paradigm are daunting for they would require the principal regional role-players to give up their present postures of confrontation and hostility, and engage with erstwhile rivals on the same platform for dialogue, establishment of confidence-building measures, and addressing of issues that divide them in a free and frank environment. Before this, the four principal Asian countries would themselves have to develop the habit of dialogue and development of consensus amongst themselves, a daunting task in itself since Asian countries have little experience of strategic dialogue with each other on Asian issues.[11]

Besides promoting Gulf security, the Asian role as a catalyst in shaping the new security architecture will have the concurrent advantage of promoting broader and deeper connectivities among the Asian producers and consumers that are not possible in a divisive political environment. These possibilities had been envisaged by then Indian Petroleum Minister Mani Shankar Aiyar, in his remarks in Beijing in January 2006, when he had set out a clear vision for Asian resurgence founded on shared energy security interests:

The Asian quest for Energy Security could lead to Asia regaining its traditional place—a place it has held for thousands of years of recorded history and lost only in the last two hundred years or so—in the vanguard of the advancement of human civilization. The Asian Renaissance brought us all to independence and liberation. Now, the Asian resurgence depends on energy cooperation in Asia. The 21st century will indeed be the Asian century only if Asian countries—buyers or sellers—join hands together in a continent-wide bid at bringing Asia together and keeping Asia together. I am confident that we will.[12]

NOTES

1. For details relating to the geology, technology and energy security implications of unconventional fuels see: Deborah Gordon, *Understanding Unconventional Oil,*: The Carnegie Endowment for International Peace, Washington DC, May 2012; Leonardo Maugeri, *Oil: The Next Revolution—The Unprecedented Upsurge of Oil Production Capacity and What it means for the World*, Belfer Centre for Science and International Affairs, Cambridge, MA, June 2012; J. David Hughes, *Drill, Baby, Drill: Can Unconventional Fuels Usher in a New Era of Energy Abundance?*, Post Carbon Institute, 2nd printing, Santa Rosa, CA, March 2013; Daniel Yergin, *The Quest—Energy, Security, and the Remaking of the Modern World*, Allen Lane, an imprint of Penguin Books, London, 2011.
2. Maria van der Hoeven, *World Energy Outlook*, International Energy Agency (IEA), Paris, April 4, 2013.
3. Dr. Hooman Peimani, "Nuclear Energy Prospects after Fukushima: The Asian Experience", Energy Studies Institute, National University of Singapore, August 28, 2012.
4. Talmiz Ahmad, "Geopolitics of West Asian and Central Asian oil and gas: Implications for India's energy security", in Ligia Noronha and Anant Sudarshan (ed), *India's Energy Security*, Routledge, London/New York, 2009, p. 69.
5. Ibid.
6. For details see: Ibid, pp. 70-73.
7. Talmiz Ahmad, "Oil diplomacy for India's energy security", in Atish Sinha and Madhup Mehta (ed), *Indian Foreign Policy: Challenges and Opportunities*, Academic Foundation, New Delhi, 2007, p. 1101-1107.
8. "Economic Outlook, analysis and forecasts: Looking to 2060—Long-term growth prospects for the world", OECD, at www.oecd.org/eco/outlook/lookingto2060.htm.
9. Dr. Mahmoud Vaezi, "Changing Asia: Toward Cooperation and a Common Identity", Centre for Strategic Research, Tehran, September 2007.
10. Bruce James, David Steven and Emily O'Brien, "Fueling a New Order? The New Geopolitical and Security Consequences of Energy", Brookings Institution, Washington DC, March 2014, p. 3.
11. For details relating to the implementation of the new Gulf security proposal, see this author's paper, "The Gulf Security Imbroglio: Shaping an Asian Initiative for a New Regional Cooperative Security Architecture", presented at the Gulf Research Meeting (GRM) 2013, University of Cambridge, July 2013. (To be published shortly.)
12. Quoted in Talmiz Ahmad, no. 4, p. 83.

6

Challenges of Indian Foreign Policy:
Post-2014 Scenario

Sudhir Singh

India became independent after a long struggle against one of the most powerful colonial powers of the contemporary world in 1947. The first Prime Minister of India Jawaharlal Nehru had two options in the immediate aftermath of independence: first, to enter into an alliance with either of the two existing blocks namely Capitalist Block led by the United States and the Communist Block led by the USSR; second, to maintain neutrality. Nehru opted for neutrality. The then contemporary international scenario had presented an extremely complex situation in the wake of the cold war. Nehru's embrace of neutrality led to the emergence of Non Aligned Movement (NAM). Although this decision have been under consistent attack and has been criticized on various counts about its failures towards not serving the cardinal purpose of national interests at several fronts. The 1962 Chinese attack was an ample proof of the adverse impact of that policy, when India was face to face with the situation akin to the theory of Prison Dilemma in international politics; i.e. either to seek the support of USA or should it align with USSR.

India could not become a strong international entity despite the strong legacy of promoter of peace, non-violence, and international brotherhood in the world during cold war era. The collapse of the USSR broadened the possibility of India acquiring a strong international image of its own. Consequently, since P.V. Narasimha Rao regime to Modi government (NDA-2) every successive regime has kept the agenda of national interest above the egalitarian agenda of idealism. The process of globalization has also been a push factor in this regard. The Pokhran-II (May 1998) further emboldened the Indian might in the realm of international politics. The whole world was compelled to concede to Indian might but not as the promoter of peace only but also as a power to be reckoned with, which could assert itself if necessary for protecting national interest and ensuring security.

However, the erstwhile dynamics of the international politics has taken a new turn after the 11 September 2001 terrorist attack on US trade center. This attack has changed the whole gamut of international politics and also proved that even the US is not safe vis-à-vis terrorist attacks. This also challenged the US claim to unipolarity in the world. The advent of multi-polarity in international politics has provided a new impetus to the emergence of India as one of the dominant poles in the foreseeable future. At the same time it has left many challenges for the formulator's of our foreign policy to cope with and respond adequately to changing situations. This paper addresses the emerging challenges for the Modi government in the wide gamut of foreign policy.

Since its inception Indian foreign policy has been obsessed with Pakistan and China. We have fought three wars with Pakistan and a fourth war by proxy/export of terrorism, which continues till date and one war with China, besides confrontations at Sikkim, Sumdorung Chu, Eastern Ladakh etc. It is also true that Pakistan has continued to try making India bleed at thousand places since the defeat of 1971 war despite all rounds efforts. Pakistan's export of terrorism is not only in Kashmir but also throughout India. Consequently, in the contemporary world Indian policy-makers have to achieve many important goals to transform India into a dominant power in the international system. It makes it imperative for Indian policy-makers to reformulate the contours of foreign policy. The first challenge before the policy-makers is to decentralize the focus (Pakistan and China) of erstwhile foreign policy and articulate the national interest in broader perspectives of the changing international scenario. Since the days of Kautilaya, maximization of national interest has remained the sole concern of foreign policy. There are no permanent friends or foes in international politics; only commonality of interests is permanent.

Narasimha Rao government launched the "Look East Policy". India is well connected with its immediate neighbour Southeast Asia on various counts. Buddhism is one of the prominent religions of this area that has its origin in India. There are enough commonalities in the field of culture too. However, there still remains a tremendous scope for more economic, technological and cultural cooperation between India and nation-states of Southeast Asia. On the ASEAN front, the Modi government has to maximize the national interests because of convergences of interests. In 2013, India-ASEAN bilateral trade was $ 80 billion, which is much bigger than expected one.[1] India and ASEAN are connected with huge landmass. Road and rail connectivity between India and ASEAN through Myanmar will give a great boost to trade. Former PM Manmohan Singh had set the time limit during November 2012 ASEAN Summit that it will be in place by March 2016. The Modi government must push this connectivity and expand already growing bilateral relations. With that connectivity India's Northeast could also become hub of commerce and result in economic emancipation, provided insurgency is assertively neutralized.

Australia is an important country by all counts and with over $ 20 billion bilateral trade, but successive Indian governments have avoided giving the required importance to it. Since the 1986 Rajiv Gandhi visits, no Indian PM has visited Australia, whereas many Australian PMs have visited India. This could well be sorted out by the Modi government. Strategic convergences are also important cementing points between India, ASEAN and Australia.

Despite consistent Pakistani cross border support to all shades of anti-national activities in India, India has exercised tremendous restraint, courage and patience. With China, which has remained India's second obsession, in spite of border problems both the countries have been converging towards building positive relations and are engaged constructively in economic exchange. Despite the legacy of hatred, the

Chinese have understood the basic fact that in post-9/11 world system the US is hell bent to encircle China and for that purpose India could be of immense importance. Given this reality in the changing parameters of the international system, the Chinese are quite intelligent to understand that they are required to keep India in good humor. During Kargil conflict (1999) both Prime Minister and Chief of Army Staff of Pakistan visited Beijing to garner Chinese support which they not only declined but even suggested to Pakistan that they could enter into dialogue with India for an ultimate solution of all outstanding issues including Kashmir.

In addition, China has already conceded that Sikkim is an integral part of India during NDA-1 regime (1998-2004) and established trade links with historic silk route passing through the Nathu La Pass and connecting Tibet. India-China had around $ 5 billion bilateral trade in the mid 1990s but within this financial year it is slated to cross $ 67 billion by 2013.[2] The Sino-Indian border problem still remains unresolved but dialogue is going on to find a solution to the same. During June 2003 Beijing visit of former PM, A.B. Vajpayee, high voltage dialogue process had been started to resolve the border problem but till July 2014 after 17 rounds, no progress has been made. In March 2013 both the Chinese PM and President changed and were replaced by a new and young team of Li and Xi. The Modi government has to do some extraordinary hard work in this domain. Chinese foreign minister visited New Delhi in the second week of June 2014 but no concrete progress could be achieved to resolve the border problem.

Our common goal must be to keep Asia multiple and for that purpose we have to allocate some structured attention towards East and North East Asia. Japan has shown its willingness to deepen relations with us. We need to respond positively and proactively. South China Sea and East China Sea issues will also need due attention of the Modi government.

Russia still remains an important global power. Without tacit understanding with Russia, India could not have succeed to establish a stable Asian order. Russia, despite the 2005 border treaty with China has apprehensions about the Chinese design in its Far East.[3] Growing

Russia-Japan relations could be seen with this prism. Although India has annual Summit level meeting arrangements, the strategic cooperation with Russia boosted by the Vajpayee-Putin meet, was targeted by the Tehelka sting operation and ten years of UPA led to much trust deficit between India and Russia. The Modi government needs to bridge that deficit and further bilateral relations. As such, Mr. Modi's visit to INS Vikramaditya, shortly after assuming charge as PM, is indeed significant.

The evolution of post-9/11 world order brought about tremendous changes in the international system which has necessitated an overhauling of our foreign policy so that we can respond to emerging new challenges. In this rapidly changing international scenario, traditional geo-politics has given way to the logic of geo-economics. Every important nation is busy to improve upon their economic profile in spite of bickering in bilateral relations. The US-China, Japan-China, ASEAN-China and India-China relations are classic examples of this argument. Both the US and China have a variety of differences but their economic relations are surging ahead. In recent years despite border disputes, India and China are also engaging and courting each other to enhance their geo-economic relations. Meanwhile, the new government needs to score on geo strategic aspects beside geo economic aspects. While China is surging rapidly, India needs to forge alliances with like minded Asian countries like Japan, South Korea, Indonesia, Vietnam etc to prevent Chinese dominance over Asia. The Modi government must make good headway with these nations.

There are some other important areas in this changing international scenario, which led to certain changes in traditional contents of India's foreign policy. The sustainable growth of Indian economy also depends on free flow of energy security because India is an energy deficit country. Energy security is a focal necessity for the sustainable growth of our country. Currently India is the 5th largest consumer of energy. It has been estimated that India would be among top three energy consuming countries superseding Russia and Japan by 2028. This expanding economy needs more energy and therefore we need to reformulate the whole energy policy keeping this reality in mind to diversify our energy supply. We are geographically close to the major sources of energy.

Unfortunately West Asia which has been traditional energy supplier to India is engulfed in violence. During 2010-11, over 57 percent of India's oil and natural gas imports came from the Gulf, principally from Saudi Arabia, Kuwait, the UAE and Iran.[4] During the same year, India's export stood $ 251 billion worth of goods while import was of $ 370 billion worth of goods, leaving India with a trade deficit of just over $ 118 billion.[5] During the same period, its energy imports stood close to $ 116 billion. The Paris based International Energy Agency estimates that India's overall dependency imports to meet net energy needs will rise from 70 percent in 2007 to 90 percent by 2030.[6] India's per capita energy consumption figure is about 520 kilograms of oil equivalent or a third of world's average.[7] Needless to say that our development is dependent on free, stable and secured supplies of the energy sources. We have immense amount of untapped water resources around us that could be also used to fill the deficit but we need diversified varieties and sources of energy to sustain our developmental process. India must diversify its energy imports from Africa, Australia, Central Asia, Myanmar, Nepal and Latin America. It will be an uphill task for the Modi government.

Another important sector is the Indian diaspora, which emerges as an important factor into post cold war international politics. We have around 27-30 million diaspora across the globe. Majority among them are settled into the powerhouse of the international system (western world) and emerged as an important determinant factor into the formulation of their respective countries' foreign policies. In 2013 India remained number one country on remittances recipient. The post 9/11 scenario has provided a new opportunity to India to exploit the situation. In the last financial year (2012-2013) our diaspora has sent maximum of remittances amounting to $ 71 billion, pushing China into third place. At the same time it is an open secret that we have not been adequately successful in safeguarding the basic interest of our diaspora, which we need to focus on with our increasing profile in the international system. Indian Diaspora is not only contributing enormously into our sustainable sound financial health but additionally they are our brilliant unpaid ambassadors situated at every corner of the globe. We need to strengthen this component of our foreign policy. This could be an important arena for the Modi government.

Science and technology is one sector in which India has achieved marvelous progress. It has provided us scope to engage with more and more countries. Right from newly emerged Central Asian Republics to poverty ridden African countries, India has tremendous scope to support their developmental work in this field. The Modi government should try to further expand this asset to more nations.

Maritime security has emerged as an important field in the emerging paradigm of foreign policy. Indian Ocean is a very important sea lane of communication through which over 80 per cent global trade traverses. Our expanding economy's sustainability needs more energy for which have to ensure maritime security. It has been said that whoever has dominated Indian Ocean has dominated Asia. Therefore we must take all possible steps to strengthen our maritime security. While India's maritime force has the capability, to only ensure its own safety but additionally also guard region against piracy it needs to be enhanced with more capacity. Besides South China and East China Seas disputes need fresh attention of the new government.

Since its inception Indian foreign policy has been obsessed with idealism which is bound to fail. India needs to reformulate the whole contours of its foreign policy. We must not get obsessed with Pakistan and China and must decentralize our attention across the globe and every region of the planet must be within our focus. There is no permanence in international relations the only thing which is permanent is commonality of interests. 2350 years back, seminal Indian strategic thinker, Kautilaya insisted on this point in an excellent manner. It is pertinent and more relevant even today and we need to incorporate it as the main determinants of our foreign policy. During cold war and post cold war period we have done many serious mistakes at the cost of our national interests. For an example, since a long time India could not take any decision on Myanmar because of its commitment for democracy and human rights. During NDA-1 regime U-turn was taken and practical engagement with military ruler was initiated. But in the meanwhile China entered deep into Myanmar and certain elements of our national interests are under threat. Replication of such a kind of steps based on ideology could be detrimental for our national interests. New government has to take care of this element in a particular manner and must sustain engaging Myanmar. Strategically it is not only well placed but is the only gateway for us for physical connectivity with ASEAN. Historically, Myanmar have been adhered by balanced foreign policy under which it has not allowed any country to dominate it, we must celebrate it and garner benefits.

Indian democracy has developed remarkably in comparison with democracies which came into being after the end of the Second World War. We have made tremendous progress at domestic level. But at the political level India has not made much progress as still for the electoral benefit political parties keep opposing or supporting foreign policy issues as per their interests. This is not a healthy trend. Political parties need to reformulate their behavior with the view that they have no difference on basic features of foreign policy and of course successive government needs to keep political parties more engaged in the process of the formulation of foreign policy. We must take some lesson from western democracies, where changing of governments has very minimal impact on the priorities of their foreign policies. 2014 elections mandate is unique because it gave majority to any single political party after 30 years. The Modi government needs to strengthen this tradition in a structured manner manifesting the courage.

In the western world, the intellectual community has been part and parcel of the formulation of foreign policy and that need to replicate into our case too. The increasing profile of India at global level has also put us into delicate situation and to cope with the situation we need to engage this class into the decision making process. The carrier diplomats are not experts of foreign policy because they have not completed any course dealing entire gamuts of foreign policy during their college/ university level. The intellectual communities are more aware about the nitty gritty of the foreign policy than the carrier diplomats and there is a strong need of their synergy for the protection and promotion of foreign policy and national interest.

Since independence Indian foreign policy has been guided by certain cardinal principles. Prime among them has been 'third world unity'. This has been one of the basic determinants of our foreign policy. Although in post cold war scenario, India has acquired enormous prestige at the international level. But with this ratio Indian engagement has not increased with the third world countries. We have been under various colonial regimes for centuries and they have exploited us blatantly and so is the case of the third world countries. Without empowering the suffering of humanities of those countries, we could not establish justice based international system. Fortunately, we have acquired tremendous development into science and technology sector. We need to develop the human development index of those hapless countries with our technological expertise and thus cement the basic unity among third world countries.

In this case the African continent is important. During our freedom struggle it was our commitment that we would bring Africa together on the path of development. Few months before our independence, Asia-Africa conference was organized at New Delhi to strengthen our common bonds. We have technological leverage at par with global status and that could be of great benefit for the African countries. We have surplus production and storage of food grains. We could supply these essential items for the survival of humanity in Africa. Africa has immense reservoir of energy. We could ensure our energy security through Africa in a bigger manner. This would be an important contribution into the establishment of justice based international system and as well in the restoration of multi-polar international system. The Modi government has to initiate some innovative projects in this regard.

Latin America has also immense important for our national interests. Instead of only developing good relations with USA only we must decentralize our energy to engage maximum countries of Latin America. This area has abundance of natural oil and gas and reservoir of other natural assets. This area is full of developing countries therefore our deepening cooperation with them could be helpful for restructuring of the international forums dominated by the west.

Another important determinant of Indian foreign policy has been decentralization of power structure into the international bodies including the United Nations. In 1945 when the UN came into being, permanent membership was extended to only five countries. With the onset of 21st century the power dynamics of the international system has changed in a dramatic manner. There is an immediate need to decentralize the UN system and the incorporation of five or ten more permanent members into the Security Council to ensure its participatory nature. India's candidature to the Security Council as the permanent member is the strongest one. India needs to shape its UN policies along this line. This is long due; Modi government is required to push the case till its logical end.

The contemporary world is confronting many burning issues, which has posed severe challenges for the humanity. Climate Change is one of the most serious among them. Developed countries have damaged the environment through their industrial waste and they have not made adequate arrangements for the safeguards. Now, entire humanity is confronting the challenges posed by the climate change. It is estimated that if corrective measures are not taken with immediate effect, the sea level will increase and all low lands will submerge. Additionally this change will create many problems and could escalate conflicts. Therefore there is strong need to explore the matter seriously. Our foreign policy must take it as one of the immediate priority because our neighborhood is going to be submerged. The developed countries that have contributed enormously to create this situation must contribute generously to the corrective measures. Likewise, eradication of poverty, removal of illiteracy and prevention of drug abuse and HIV/AIDS must be tackled effectively and swiftly as these are possible factors of conflicts throughout the world. While the international community must take these challenges seriously, the Modi government needs to initiate many new initiatives to solicit south-south cooperation in dealing with these challenges.

Another major challenge for the Modi government will be Afghanistan. Engulfed in violence since the last three and half decades, by the end of 2014 when the NATO forces are intended to withdraw, the security scenario in Afghanistan and its vicinity will further deteriorate. Pakistan will try its level best to dominate Afghanistan and erase the leverage which India has achieved since the last one decade. India will face the heat not only in Kashmir but across the country. Already, Pakistani Taliban and other terrorist groups there as well as Al Qaeda and others in Afghanistan will be further emboldened to strike in India, Pakistan and Afghanistan.

Therefore Modi government needs to reformulate its strategy to contain the situation and ensure national security. Kautilya, one of the oldest realists in the realm of foreign policy advocated peace. According to him "peace should always be preferred to war; 'When the degree of progress is the same in pursuing peace and waging war, peace is to be preferred'. For, in war, there are many disadvantages, such as the loss of troops, expenditure and absence from home."[8] Indian culture also promotes peace and global peace, but peace should not be at the cost of self respect. Kautilaya states "However, the main target of the conqueror is always the designated natural enemy; one cannot make peace with an enemy."[9]

One more urgent requirement is removal of slow mentality of our bureaucracy. There is hardly any deal which India has inked with different countries that has been completed within the stipulated time-frame. The need of the hour is to fix the accountability and implement the projects within their due dates.

These are the broader issues that need immediate attention of the Modi government. With the passage of time requirements may change and to cope with to these challenges new and relevant formulations and implementations of policies are an urgent primary requisite. These steps will be the onus of the new government to promote and protect India's national interests.

Prime Minister, Narendra Modi invited all SAARC members to witness his swearing in and despite domestic protests they attended. Through this process Modi government has shown that it intendeds to ensure sustainable development along with the neighbors. SAARC countries through their participation vowed their willingness to extent their support to this noble diplomacy of the Modi government. Modi's choice of Bhutan as his first foreign destination also vindicates his urge to strengthen the relations with the SAARC countries. It could be safely said on the basis of the performance of the Modi government that its beginning has been good but the serious challenge is to sustain the process. With a huge mandate and determination, it would not be impossible for the Modi government to not only ensure national interests but to establish India as a global power, as dreamt by Vinayak Damodar Savarkar, the important ideologue of the RSS. Savarkar, maintained that a strong national identity as ultimately necessary for a strong national military. In his view, a shared national identity gives soldiers something to fight for and those with a strong sense of identity will always fight better than those without.

During NDA-1 rule, former PM Vajpayee was very keen to promote national interests in the realm of foreign policy. In Modi's own words, Vajpayee demonstrated an ability to maneuver Indian foreign policy between *shanti* (peace) and *shakti* (power).

Kautilya stated that 'The welfare of the state depends on an active foreign policy.' The contours of security in contemporary world—Asia-Pacific in particular and the globe in general—are changing rapidly. India has been provided with a golden opportunity of a possibility of achieving these cardinal goals. Of course, enormous diplomatic efforts, vision and statesmanship will be the fundamental challenges for the Modi government.

NOTES AND REFERENCES

1. *Annual Report,* Ministry of External Affairs, New Delhi, 2013, p. 11.
2. Ibid, p. 9.
3. Karaganor, Sergei, "Russia's Asian Strategy," *Russia in Global Affairs,* July 2, 2011.
4. P.R. Kumaraswamy, *Persian Gulf 2012: India's Relations with the Region,* New Delhi; MEI@ND, 2012, www.mei.org.in.
5. Director General of Foreign Trade Data Bank, http//commerce.nic.in/eidb/default.asp.
6. *World Energy Outlook,* 2007, Paris; International Energy Agency, 2007, p. 495.
7. Tanvi Madan, *The Brookings Foreign Policy Studies Energy Security Series*; India; Washington DC; The Brookings Institution, 2006, p. 9.
8. Rangrajan, *Kautilya The Arthashastra,* Penguin, New Delhi, 1992, p. 512.
9. Ibid, p. 512.

7

What Should be Modi's Foreign Policy?

Pankaj Jha

With a number of psephologists predicting a possible formation of a Narendra Modi government, it needs to be assessed that what could be possible challenges in case Narendra Modi becomes the future Prime Minister of India. The calls for a rising and shining India need to be reaffirmed with a proactive India in the foreign policy circles. The concentric circles approach that Indian foreign policy has steadfastly adopted in the last decade needs further calibration and articulation in terms of diplomatic priorities and strategic outlook. The need for analysing Kautilaya's '*Mandala*' and the search for strategic partners at the international forums need to be taken up again. Moreover, the biggest challenge that the new PM would have to face will be with regard to the nations along the western border of India, primarily Pakistan and Afghanistan. The US drawdown from Afghanistan would mean that India will have to undertake a Strength, Weakness, Opportunities and Threats (SWOT) analysis for its own internal security and regional security.

The countries in West Asia are also apprehensive about the hardliner *Hindutva* government coming to the fore and the status of Muslims in such a governance structure. The energy supplies and the better cordial relations with Muslim majority countries would be at test for regional politics and diplomatic adroitness for the incumbent government. While it is true that the UPA government might not have configured its foreign policy because of the recurrent changes in the cabinet portfolios, it should be acknowledged that UPA has very deftly balanced its relations with West Asia and Israel, both at the same time. Iran, despite severe sanctions, has remained one of the important suppliers of crude oil to India while Saudi Arabia cooperated through repatriating the wanted Indian terrorists from the Kingdom. However, India's convenient long silence on critical international issues, be it the case of Syria or for that matter prosecution of Rohingyas in Myanmar might have projected a nation of 1.2 billion people as lacking the political will and over cautious diplomatic core. Any further ambiguous stance on foreign policy issues would project India as a reluctant player in international politics. This paper outlines the emerging challenges for new incumbent government.

South Asia: Fig Leaf to the Neighbours

For any new incumbent government the main challenge would be to improve relations with its immediate neighbourhood including Pakistan, Bangladesh, Nepal, Sri Lanka, Maldives and Myanmar. With Pakistan, the relations have improved but there are hardly any tangible results on the ground with Pakistan playing a reluctant role in giving India the Most Favoured Nation (MFN) status and also not taking enough measures to prosecute the perpetrators of the 2008 Mumbai Terror attacks. However, the cross-border infiltration and Pakistan's support to the transnational terror groups is what the new government would have to take head on and must have to create pockets of positive constituencies which can lobby on behalf of India. Moreover, India would need to sensitise the nongovernmental organisations, primarily international ones, so as to create a positive approach. More importantly, the media channels which have used the India's human rights record to pitch in for their foreign equity holders should abhor the anti-government and anti-institution stance and in case these do not comply then these must be asked to wind up their operations in India. Media freedom cannot be subservient to a nation's sovereignty. The new government would have to provide the carrot-and-stick policy with Pakistan. On the one hand India should make it clear that any further terror attacks in the Indian heartland would be dealt with the surgical strikes across the border and on the other, any cooperative gesture would translate into across the board trade and economic benefits. This would mean easy visa procedures for short-term visits, family visas and also business visas for those who have been vetted by the Indian High Commission in Islamabad.

Modi will have to deal with the arrest of Indian fisherman across the international waters and must make a Standard Exchange Procedures (SEP) for the release of such fishermen and their boats, the only livelihood of these poor fisherman. Moreover, India will have to work out a set timelines for result in of the Sir Creek maritime border issues. This would mean reaching an agreed settlement without dragging the issue for another decade. In this regard the stakeholders should be taken into confidence.

With regard to Nepal which has held successful elections last year, there is need for reinvigoration of the ties. The effort should be made to reduce Chinese influence in Nepal and accelerating better economic benefits to the Nepalese manufacturers and traders. Moreover, the Indian government should initiate Track I and II talks with all the stakeholders involved in the formation of a new constitution in the Himalayan kingdom. As Nepal has already been provided with a land transit route, there is need for joint venture and electricity projects so as to cater to the people on both sides of the international border.

Bhutan has also been wooed by China and even though each nation has every right to engage its neighbours at all levels—diplomatically, politically and economically; there should not be the case where India's loss becomes China's gain. Bhutan needs further investment from India and this should be done at all levels after due feasibility studies have been done. Bhutan being the happiest nation on earth needs prosperity and development as well as training of its diplomatic and military personnel so that it can emerge as the Switzerland of Asia.

With Sri Lanka, it has been observed from certain quarters that the coalition politics has taken a toll on the bilateral ties but many nations have observed that a better dialogue with Sri Lanka would go a long way in rehabilitating the Tamils and also provide them the necessary employment and housing facilities. Those Tamil-dominated areas need a representation in the form of provincial councils and district administration so that the decade lost in the war could be recovered. Sri Lanka being the member of Commonwealth should be provided with necessary military aid and assistance sop that it need not have to scout for military equipment from India's neighbours such as China and Pakistan.

While relations with Bangladesh have improved a lot but in terms of trade and investment there is a need for acceleration. Moreover, Bangladesh and India need to resolve the water sharing agreement and should join hands to negotiate with China on the dams which have been under construction in China. Bangladesh political parties need an effective two-way communication with the Indian establishment and this should be ensured. Further, there is need for PM envoys to all the South Asian countries and these must not be diplomats because the retired diplomats come with their own lifetime prejudices. In fact, academics from Kolkata and Delhi should be elevated to act as envoys.

With Maldives, the new government has been positively disposed towards India. During his visit to India in January 2014, Maldivian President Abdulla Yameen stated that its ties with China "very close" but pitching India at a higher level he said that India is "far more precious". India needs to reformat its ties with Maldives and undertake development and capacity building programmes with the new government. More importantly, India should engage in health and education in Maldives. The aid and assistance that India has provided in the last few years have been appreciated in Maldivian society but it needs to be reinforced with continued commitment to the cause of the island nation.

China: The Policy Enigma

With China incrementally raising its military spending and also inundating the Indian market with goods that are cheap but are at the same time decimating the domestic manufacturing might not augur well for Indian economy in the long run. For example, Indian silk and toy industry have suffered maximum because of cheap, substandard Chinese goods. The imbalances in trade need to be conveyed firmly and advocacy for Indian services export should be made with the Chinese establishment. Moreover, in the past incidents of misbehaviour against Indian businessmen have vitiated the atmosphere between the two nations and India must make stringent guidelines for its own businessmen involved in dubious transactions and fraud. Further, a dispute settlement mechanism should be in place for resolving trade and other related issues. Also, Chinese authorities should be conveyed that any mistreatment would be met with complete blockade of merchandise trade. Until and unless, Modi government does not take these initiatives, the sound of assertive India would not resonate in Chinese policy circles. It is well known in many international forums that China only caters to the assertive countries.

However, China should not be demonised to the extent of vitiating the atmosphere and creating unnecessary tensions between the two nations. Modi must make a strong pitch for resolving the territorial issue with China on a priority basis. The middle sector boundary demarcation could be the good starting point. Also, there is a need for strict adherence to the confidence building and basic guidelines for resolving border issues between the two sides. Indian market should be the strong point of negotiations with China, and Modi government must make a strong advocacy for these. Many strategic commentators have called for greater Chinese investment but if Chinese outward FDI are analysed, its investments in Southeast Asia, South Asia and Africa has been very miniscule. Therefore, India might not even ask for Chinese investment which is very meagre. Moreover, China does not want any competitive manufacturing centres in and around its periphery. In terms of China's assertive behaviour in multilateral forums and even its attempts to outwit India must be met with adroitness and Indian diplomacy is capable enough for these but lacks the political support. Modi will have to provide not only succour to the military forces but also stand with the diplomatic core. The point of reference should be post nuclear testing phase in 1998 when India's diplomacy and military preparedness were at the peak. However, in order to achieve the strategic teeth, Modi government would have to make amends to the defence acquisition. The media should also not play into the hands of foreign vendors who have lost in the tendering process.

US: The Unpredictable Partner

With US, India has maintained a strategic relation which has turned out to be a strategic equation. The two countries need to work on solving this strategic equation so that it becomes once again a strategic solution for India's interests and US approach towards India. The Devyani Khobargade case and the trade issue have lingered long in the strategic psyche of India. Both countries need to come over these difficult issues. Moreover, with the resignation of US Ambassador Nancy Powell, it seems that the US is keen on enhancing ties with India, especially when countries such as Canada and UK have taken a leap ahead of US diplomacy in terms of engaging Narendra Modi. The resolve of the NDA government in the past to give necessary momentum to the trade and economic ties might very well need to be reinvigorated. The meeting of the EU delegation with Modi underscored the need of a strong economic denominator for long lasting strategic marriage. However, while Indian market is a very lucrative incentive, it must not be done at the cost of job losses. The fine balance need to be maintained so that India gains in terms of trade quota and opening up of services industry in US. The high visa charges and the limited number of H-I visas need to be addressed by the new incumbent government. Moreover, in terms of lifting of sanctions and high technology imports from US, there are still a number of hindrances and if US wants to add India as a true strategic partner, it needs to show the connect and resolve in enhancing ties.

Russia: Time Tested Friend

With Russia, the support extended to the country in the Ukraine crisis shows that India would always count on Russia, a long-time friend. However, Russia also needs to take a liberal approach in certain trade and investment issues with India. Moreover, India's security needs have been rising and Russia needs to offer a priority treatment to India in energy exploration projects, especially in Sakhalin blocks. India and Russia have engaged each other in a number of forums and Russia needs to understand that while China is a rising power, India is a liked power. For the Modi government, the challenge would be to streamline R&D projects in India, especially in military and defence weapon systems (for example in fifth generation fighter programme and stealth fighter development, Brahmos Hyper sonic missile systems and beyond range radar systems) and also address the grouse that Russia has been nurturing that India is getting uncomfortably close to US. For India, the tests would be to get into the Shanghai Cooperation Organisation (SCO) and also enhance relations with the Central Asia republics which have been very warm to India's initiatives in those countries. Given the fact that India has not nurtured any expansionist intentions, the time has come for India to capitalise on its soft power and engage the countries even in China's periphery without any 'what-China-will-think' guilt clouding their larger national interest. Russia has been supportive of India's gestures in the former CIS countries and there is a need to engage Russia in Afghanistan and other regional spheres also.

West Asia: The Policy Quagmire

For the Modi government, the 'thorn in the throne' would be the relations with West Asia. As already a sizeable number of Indian Diaspora, out of which a large majority are Muslims have conveyed their apprehensions to the larger population in West Asia, in case Modi ascends to power. This issue would need to be addressed on a priority basis. Modi government needs to prioritise its relations with the major nations in the region along with the prime financial centres. Moreover, the impending frictions between Saudi Arabia and Iran would lead the new government to some unpleasant choices. It must be recalled that Iran has sustained energy exports to India despite international sanctions and India in turn has withstood international pressure to buy the Iranian oil. Saudi Arabia has also showed a keenness to engage India and the deportation of Indian terrorist from the Kingdom (as per one estimate more than 12 terrorists have been deported in the last two years). This act of Saudi kingdom needs to be appreciated because it withstood Pakistani establishment's pressure to connect to India. India also needs to connect to its large Indian Diaspora (more than 6 million) who have been contributing to the Indian economy through large sums of remittances. However, in terms of strong labour employment schemes and stipulations adopted by both Saudi Arabia and Kuwait, India needs to address these issues and make it a point that India's labourers are not maltreated in the Kingdom and elsewhere in the Gulf region.

The one concern which might resonate in the larger policy circles is the increase in radical elements among Indian expatriates in the Gulf population. As already a number of Indian expatriates labour have also come along with very radical thinking, clearly undermining the basic tenets of Indian Islamic thinking which is more liberal and *Sufi* oriented. This needs to be addressed but before that India needs to release innocent Muslims lodged in jails across the country but it must make no amends to the terrorists who have been trying to destroy the secular fabric of the nation. Modi must make a visit to any of these Gulf nations to show that his resolve is 'India and Indians first' without mincing words.

East Asia: Incremental Approach is not the Way Ahead

India has engaged the northeast Asia countries in a big way and it is apparent in the security partnership with Japan and the larger Strategic partnership with Korea; not to mention India does have fairly good diplomatic relations with North Korea. While Japan has been keen on engaging India in the strategic sphere and also engages in the bilateral exercises, India has adopted a rather subdued approach. India under Modi should engage the economic heavyweights in the region so as to have double benefits, both in terms of economic exchanges and enhancement of trade as well as defence imports from these technologically advanced countries. With Japan, India must engage the country in terms of developing better Sonar systems; develop submarine warfare capability and enhancing its maritime surveillance and communication systems. Japan has been appalled at the lack of policy directions and inertia in India owing to the bureaucratic wrangles and lack of political will to engage Japan. However, there has been incremental change but for long-term policy shift there needs to be tectonic political will.

Indian Diaspora: Connect, Collate and Engage

In the Modi government, Indian Diaspora is expected to play a critical role, be it the case of engaging US or for that matter investing in the country. However, in the past Indian Diaspora has not benefitted much through its investments because of the lack of single window clearing systems and the unnecessary clearances that are required for setting up any manufacturing unit. In fact, Indian Diaspora should be given a priority in terms of investment in the country. Further, India must engage its Diaspora more methodically through creating Diaspora pools of talent which can assist Indian in terms of policy formulation and also discussing India's approach to the wider international community. Nevertheless, there still exist a wind of caution as in the past a number of strong ethnic Indians have taken up the mantle of leaders of Indian Diaspora and this should be discouraged. India needs to connect to its younger Diaspora, not the political leaders having very little or negligible clout in host country.

Further, there is need for constituting another Diaspora Committee, because, L.M. Singhvi Committee Report submitted in 2001 has done commendable job and there is need to refresh the data as well as information about Indian Diaspora. Indian foreign ministry needs to constitute another committee to look into the Indian Diaspora, their grievances and their achievements in host countries. Modi must ask Indian Diaspora to return to the roots and must provide two years multiple entry visas for them to contribute to the Indian economy.

Conclusion

For the Modi government, in terms of foreign policy articulation and projection, the task would be arduous but not impossible. First and foremost, Modi government would have to activate its resources and personnel in foreign countries. It must communicate the sense of proactive India which has the political will to undertake responsibilities and project its image in the larger international forums. This needs to be done with a planning and proper policy articulation. India must come out with a Defence White Paper and Strategic Policy paper which would articulate its projections for the future. Moreover, the stern message that Modi gives at times exudes confidence and it should be maintained. A benign India is accepted but an irrelevant India is not beneficial to the Indian interests and also its international standing. Secondly, there is a need for collating all intellectual capital which is young and dynamic and has the potential to take India forward. A rather toned down approach and also lack of initiative would mar India's interests be it the case of UN Security Council permanent membership or for that matter its standing in a number of international institutions. Thirdly, India should, under Modi, accelerate the negotiations for a number of Free Trade Agreements but at the same time should negotiate for services trade and investment protection agreements, and dispute settlement mechanism should be addressed simultaneously. Fourthly, India must make its terms and conditions for engagement with the major powers and should stay firm with regard to its strategic autonomy but conditional support on international issues which benefit only India. After all, what Modi professes is India first and it must resonate in its foreign policy projection.

8

Rapid Urbanisation Posing Huge Infrastructure Challenges

Sudipt Arora

With 1.2 billion people and the world's fourth-largest economy, India is now facing a rare window of opportunity to improve quality of life for its citizens and lay foundations for a prosperous future that will impact generations to come.

Historic changes are unfolding and unleashing a host of new opportunities. India will soon have the largest and youngest workforce the world has ever seen. At the same time, the country is witnessing a massive wave of urbanisation with about 10 million people moving to towns and cities each year in search of jobs and opportunity.

The World Bank describes it as the largest rural-urban migration of this century. Massive investments will be needed to create the jobs, housing, and infrastructure to meet soaring aspirations and make towns and cities more livable and green.

Generating inclusive growth will be key as more than 400 million people—or one-third of the world's poor—still live in poverty. On the other hand, the country's infrastructure needs are massive. One in three rural people lack access to an all-weather road, and only one in five national highways is four-lane. Ports and airports have inadequate capacity. Trains move very slowly.

Some 300 million people do not have access to electricity, and those who do face frequent disruptions. A country aspiring to become economic superpower on the global horizon surely deserves a better deal.

Rapid Urbanisation

India's urban sprawl is poised to become second largest in the world with more people living in cities than in many countries. The number of cities with one million to four million people will increase from 48 to 68 in the next two decades.

Already the country has nine with a population of more than four million people each. By 2030, the number will go up to 13. Six cities—Delhi, Mumbai, Kolkata, Chennai, Bengaluru and Pune—will have more than 10 million people each by then.

The total urban population is 380 million and may exceed the earlier projection of 590 million by 2030. Rapid urbanisation should prompt policymakers to create surpluses rather than managing shortages.

It is well known that mistakes in urban development cannot be changed for centuries—especially in a democratic country like ours. The role of private sector is crucial and the government should restrict its role to policymaking and regulating.

Rapid economic growth and a young population with an average age of 29 years will need 70 new cities by 2020, of which 20 should have been in advanced planning stages by now. That is not happening. As a result, there is crumbling urban infrastructure that calls for radical solutions.

There is urgent need for better governance and restructuring of civic bodies for speedy urban development process across the country.

Mass-transit Rail Systems

Developing mass-transport systems in major cities is imperative to reduce vehicular population on roads. The national capital has 7 million vehicles while another million come in every day from surrounding cities.

Developing housing structures for the city's burgeoning population too has also been a challenge for many governments in the past half century. The supply has not kept up with the rising demand. There is need to change land laws and building laws that were made in 1895.

Already, 80 per cent of the 170 billion dollars in tax revenue collected by the government comes from urban areas. This will rise to 892 billion dollars or 85 per cent in the next 20 years. There will be critical political impact of this urbanisation that should be studied by all stakeholders.

A major metro rail network is thus a necessity for future urbanisation as India moves rapidly into 21st century's new economic infrastructure with its industrial and service economy overshadowing farming economy as the main driver of GDP.

The big challenge for urban planners is to cope up with seven mega cities with 20 per cent of India's population and demanding 40 per cent of total investments projected. Investment requirements for urban transport development in 87 cities are estimated at 80 billion dollars.

Changing GDP Composition

Rapid GDP growth has dramatically raised the share of industry and services in the Indian economy. Agriculture accounted for 52 per cent of GDP in 1950 and 29.5 per cent as recently as 1990. This is now down to just 14 per cent.

From the perspective of 21st century, we have to accept urbanisation as an inevitable consequence of the emergence of an industry and service driven economy. The transformation in Indian economy has been straight into services which now constitute more than 56 per cent of GDP content.

The tradition of 70 per cent of the people depending upon agriculture that contributes less than 15 per cent of GDP can only perpetuate large swathes of the population remaining at low levels of income and well-being.

Less than one-third of population currently lives in urban areas. For many reasons including the fact that rural India cannot find adequate income-generating jobs, to the rising rural population, migration of population to urban areas has been going on in the six decades since Independence in 1947.

This reality, along with industrialisation in hinterland areas, has led to the creation of new towns and swollen the existing cities to unacceptable levels of growth. As a result, slums now account for one-quarter of all urban housing.

In certain top metropolitan areas such as Mumbai, almost half the population is estimated to live in slums or unauthorised colonies without any basic amenities—mainly because these habitations are near their work areas or where unorganised jobs are available.

Labour Pains

India represents the single largest pool of young, potentially skilled labour in the world with about one-third of its people below the age of 15 and only five percent above 65.

The country has 17 per cent of the world's population—more than the United States, Indonesia, Brazil, Pakistan and Bangladesh combined. The increase between 2001 and 2011 was 181 million, roughly equivalent to the entire population of Brazil.

By 2030, experts expect India to overtake China with 1.3 billion people as the world's most populous nation. But only 39 people out of every 100 in India are employed.

Equipping the workforce with the right skills presents significant challenges to developing countries with large populations. Senior government officials and industry leaders fear the country's much-lauded economic growth could be in danger because there are not enough people to build India Inc.

Despite its huge working-age population, the country faces a potentially debilitating shortage of skilled workers. Only 5 per cent of India's 400 million strong labour force has received any formal training compared with 70 per cent in Germany and 95 per cent in South Korea.

As a result of this shortage, property development companies—to name just one industry—have been compelled to import architects, designers and planners from countries such as Thailand, Singapore, China, Australia and New Zealand on handsome salaries, thereby pushing up project costs and affecting profitability.

Though millions of Indians remain unemployed or underemployed, the country's lagging bricks-and-mortar industries have imported tens of thousands of foreign workers—on business visas, no less—to build and operate power plants, steel mills and telecommunications towers.

The Delhi airport was built by Chinese labour. There are many examples of India's efforts to improve its dismal infrastructure. We can't wait. In the next two to three years we have to put in place a skills training capacity of at least 40 million people a year.

Skill Development

Across the board, the shortage of skilled labourers has reduced productivity and cut into profits. Poaching workers from competitors has become a common practice that drives up wages, threatening to derail India's manufacturing revolution before it has even begun.

The crux of the problem is that India has never really industrialised. India's service-related businesses account for more than half of GDP while manufacturing contributes only 15 per cent.

And though China's economy is only four times larger than India's, its manufacturing sector is 50 times larger. Meanwhile, China has some 500,000 vocational training centres, compared with India's 10,000 obsolete Industrial Training Institutes.

More than 90 per cent of India's workforce is still employed in the so-called unorganised sector with no social security benefits. Where neither safety standards nor minimum wage laws can be enforced, nor is there is any money for boots and hardhats. There is surely none for technology or training.

It varies a lot by sector, but we are seeing shortages anecdotally in several areas. In some cases it is constraining growth, and in some cases it is increasing the cost of doing business. At the current capacity, we'll be able to train about 50 million people in 10 years versus the 500 million we need to train. So there's a severe shortage.

By 2020 India's construction industry will need 33 million more skilled crane operators, electricians, welders, masons and so on; the textile and clothing industry will need 26 million loom and sewing machine operators; automobile and auto parts manufacturing industries will need 35 million machinists, mechanics and other positions.

The construction industry—one of the most critical drivers of growth in India with a compound annual growth rate of 12 per cent—will need five million civil engineers, architects and planners but the country is expected to produce fewer than one million of these professionals.

There is big money at stake. The government is planning to invest 100 billion dollars in infrastructure over the next three years, which means huge deals for construction companies.

Managing Skill Shortages

The World Bank said in a recent report that India had about 110,000 highway engineers. China, by comparison, had five times that number when it started to modernise its road infrastructure in the 1990s.

In biotechnology, there is a need for 80 per cent more scientists with doctorates. In banking and finance in 2006, there is a 90 per cent shortage of risk managers; 65 per cent for tech professionals, 50 per cent for treasury managers, 75 per cent for credit operations professionals and 80 per cent for financial analysts.

The tech sector is expected to face a shortage of as many as 500,000 employees this year. In sectors such as technology and financial services, there's plenty of moving around because of the number of opportunities available as companies ramp up aggressively.

But in newer sectors such as real estate, retailing and private equity, there aren't enough people in the market with relevant experience.

The economy has expanded at an average annual rate of more than 8.5 per cent since 2003, and sectors such as technology and IT services have grown at a double-digit pace. India churns out about 2.5 million college and university graduates each year, including 400,000 engineers, but the numbers are misleading.

The number of graduates is small relative to the size of the population —about 10 per cent of Indians receive any college training, as opposed to 50 per cent in the United States—and the quality of their education is often doubtful.

A recent industry study found that only a quarter of the graduates churned out each year are fit to be employed by foreign and Indian tech companies. Problems include a lack of English-speaking skills and the absence of standardised curricula and programmes that provide graduates with technical skills.

A software major found only 2 per cent of the 1.3 million job applicants it reviewed last year acceptable. There's a lack of workers even at the lower rungs in industries such as mining, food processing and textiles. The reasons include working hours that are unsatisfactory to prospective employees, distant locations and a dearth of sector-specific skills.

In short, India's aspirations of boosting manufacturing output to 25 per cent of GDP by 2025—creating 100 million jobs and bringing hundreds of millions more people out of poverty in the process – may well hang in the balance.

Good Governance Must

Recent general elections have shown whichever government does not perform is going to be voted out of power. There is young and impatient India out here demanding good governance essential to ensure full benefits of various policy interventions.

We need ideas. We need capacity to turn those ideas into policies and programmes. And we need boldness and a sense of purpose to implement those policies and programmes.

Output and capacity creation targets in crucial infrastructure sectors like coal, power and roads may be fulfilled. There should be greater clarity on issues relating to land acquisition and environment.

Necessary steps must be taken to revitalise traditional crop agriculture which is vital to food security and farm income. The last two years have clearly shown how a decline in agricultural production can cause serious distortions in the economy. It is therefore imperative that we aim at GDP originating from agriculture and allied activities growing at four per cent per annum.

The second challenge is shortage of physical infrastructure of which the single most important item is electricity. A more aggressive path of capacity creation must start immediately. Constraints such as availability of coal, land acquisition and environmental issues need to be tackled so that the desired growth in capacity expansion can be achieved.

As India moves to a higher trajectory of economic growth, it must sustain a high growth rate of eight to nine over the next two decades to substantially raise the living standards of people. Growth must lead to reduction of poverty and the process of growth must be broad- based to include all segments of society.

We must expand employment opportunities and improve productivity in all sectors of the economy. We must narrow economic disparities across and within the states. And, finally, we must improve on social indicators.

India's economy, Asia's third-largest, is largely driven by domestic demand. High inflation, rising interest rates and high crude oil prices are a matter of concern. The new dispensation at Raisina Hills in New Delhi must realise that what we need is good infrastructure for the industry to grow fast.

9

Too Much on the Political, Diplomatic Plate for the BJP

Tripti Nath

The Indian National Congress, the grand old party which dates back to the late 19th century and ruled for about five-sixth of the 67 years from the time India won Independence in 1947, was decimated in the recently concluded elections in the world's largest democracy.

As expected, the magic of dynastic politics worked little for Congress which had no choice but to accept its worst poll tally of 44 seats out of the total 543 Parliamentary constituencies. The Congress President, Mrs. Sonia Gandhi and her son, Mr. Rahul Gandhi managed to save their family seats of Rae Bareilly and Amethi respectively. Thank God for small mercies! So, what really went wrong despite the Congress working overtime in its war room to set the house in order and project Congress Vice President Rahul Gandhi, the great grandson of Jawaharlal Nehru, India's first Prime Minister, as its leader?

The election results clearly reflected the verdict that represented the choice of 814 million electors who voted for political stability. After three decades, the nation witnessed the emergence of a single largest party.

At the very start of the election year, Mr Narendra Modi, who was then the Chief Minister of Gujarat had declared at the 'Sankalp' rally in Panaji, that the Congress has taken India 50 years back. For this, he held the people and the parties who support the Congress as equally responsible. So, what really did not work for the Congress in this election merits scrutiny.

The writing was on the wall for quite some time and the Congress strategy of a third term in power was clearly flawed. The then Prime Minister Dr. Manmohan Singh rarely spoke. His integrity was tainted by a series of financial scandals and his passive attitude had an adverse impact on his credibility. His hands were tied as the real power centre was 10, Janpath ruled by the United Progressive Alliance Chairperson Sonia Gandhi. The icing on the cake was that the Congress failed to project Rahul Gandhi as its Prime Ministerial candidate and on being cornered by the media, said that it never had a tradition of naming a PM candidate. In contrast, the BJP's announcement of Mr Narendra Modi as its Prime Ministerial candidate gave the party a head start. Apart from anti incumbency, what worked wonders for the BJP was a serious leadership crisis in the Congress. In this scenario, the disillusioned Indian voters saw Mr Modi as a rising star who took care to leave no pressing concerns unaddressed in his rallies. Whether it was the cause of the "jawan" (soldier) and "kisan" or farmers suicides, poverty or price rise, a hardline approach on Pakistan, Mr Modi voiced concern on all burning issues.

He enjoyed the backing of businessmen and successful non resident Indians who were keen that he replicate his Gujarat state model of good roads, 24/7 electricity and less red tape.

The anti incumbency hard-to-shake off load of 10 years, was dominated by numerous challenges on the domestic front including unendurable price rise, economic disparity, farmers suicides despite the farm loan waiver scheme of Rs 71,000 crore announced by the Congress led UPA government in 2008, rampant corruption, criminals in politics and unacceptable cases of violence against women.

In the 17 years gone by, about three lakh farmers ended their lives and the survival of many other farmers is uncertain. Their families have been facing poverty for generations. Its about time policy makers prioritised pressing concerns in the social sector.

A country that boasts of self reliance in space may first do well to provide basic civic amenities to its citizens. These statistics may serve as a wake up call. Fifty per cent of Indians don't have proper shelter, 70 per cent don't have access to decent toilets, 35 per cent households don't have a water source nearby, 85 per cent villages don't have a secondary school and more than 40 per cent of the same villages don't have proper road connectivity.

In the second term of Congress led UPA, the government has had to face several diplomatic problems in dealing with Pakistan, China, United States and ironically, Italy, where the Congress president hails from. In 2013, two Indian soldiers were beheaded and mutilated during clashes at the Kashmir border. The same year, there were no less than 18 face-offs between Indian and Chinese troops in Pangong Tso due to serious differences in perception on the LAC and due to massive Chinese infrastructure build-up close to the line. The intrusions continue. Just two days before the Indian Vice President Hamid Ansari's visit to Beijing and Xian, Chinese troops intruded into the Indian territory in the Ladakh region of Jammu and Kashmir on June 24. They stayed out for over two hours before being pushed by the Indian side. During his election campaign, Modi had criticised China's expansionist foreign policy but the hard fact is that China continues to make territorial claims over India with frequent border intrusions. Both countries signed a Border Defence Cooperation Agreement on October 23, 2013, seeking to facilitate ways and means to implement border defence cooperation; measures to facilitate contacts and to enhance understanding and cooperation between the border defence forces as well as procedures to be followed where there is no common understanding of the Line of Actual Control.

The Agreement strengthens maintenance of stability on the border and adds to existing instruments to ensure peace and stability on our borders. During his recent visit to India, the Chinese Foreign Minister said that the boundary question is a difficult one but both countries will eventually find a solution with strong will and resolve.

Although the Chinese Foreign Minister Wang Yi's two day visit to India as a special envoy of President Xi Jinping in the first month of Mr

Modi's assuming charge signals a desire to normalise ties, one cannot lose sight of the fact that relations between the two fastest growing economies have not been so rosy in the past. Against the backdrop of frequent intrusions, it would be somewhat difficult for the new regime to make a sound judgment on economic convergence but it ought to work on the optimism expressed by Mr Yi on the boundary question.

India needs to pay equal attention to address irritants in its relations with the United States and its immediate neighbours Sri Lanka and Pakistan. Relations between India and Sri Lanka are under strain due to fishermen straying into each other's waters. In 2013 alone, 626 Indian fishermen were arrested and 200 Sri Lankan fishermen were arrested. The Indian leadership also needs to ensure that the Sri Lankan Tamils achieve socio political and economic equality.

And now issues related to Pakistan. While Modi who did not pull his punches on Pakistan in many of his widely attended pre election speeches, he raised many an eyebrow by extending a hand of friendship to Pakistan by inviting the Pakistan Prime Minister to his oath taking ceremony. Mr Sharif graced the occasion and his government reciprocated with a humanitarian gesture by releasing 152 fishermen, most of who came from Gujarat. But both countries need to work on this bonhomie further, reduce trust deficit caused by years of hostility and suspicion and address all comprehensive issues as Kashmir, Siachen and water sharing. The two sides are currently preparing to discuss a new roadmap for trade liberalisation. To put an end to perpetual hostility, both sides must make sincere efforts for sustainable peace.

Even as diplomatic channels in India and United States were making guesses about the direction in which India US relations were headed, the new BJP regime gave out a clear message of tough diplomacy, barely five weeks after taking charge. Reacting to reports that America's National Security Agency was authorised to snoop on BJP in 2010, the Ministry of External Affairs summoned a top US diplomat to raise the issue and categorically convey that it was "totally unacceptable that an Indian organisation or Indian individual's privacy was transgressed upon." India did not stop at this. It went on to seek an assurance that such a thing would not recur. It remains to be seen how India's stand will affect the outcome of the talks between the US President Barack Obama and our Prime Minister during the bilateral summit level talks in Washington scheduled in September end.

The US efforts to reach out to Modi before he came to steer India, deserves a mention here. As soon as a watchful United States noticed Modi inching towards the much coveted 7, Race Course official residence, it declared that he would be granted a visa to visit the United States if he were elected Prime Minister. By doing so, it lifted the revocation of Modi's US visa by the State Department in 2005 on the ground that he didn't do enough to prevent the Gujarat riots a few years earlier. President Obama called Modi and invited him to visit Washington. This change in tone in Washington towards India is welcome given the fact that much pessimism had crept into India US relations especially after the arrest of Indian diplomat Devyani Khobragade in New York in December 2013 on visa fraud charges. The relations had also been plagued by other factors as India's refusal to recognise intellectual property rights of some US based pharmaceutical companies, lack of progress in implementing the civil nuclear treaty and an overall policy paralysis is New Delhi.

News reports from US indicate that Modi's elevation as Prime Minister has led to newfound optimism in the business community in US which is confident given its past experience of dealing with Narendra Modi when he was the Chief Minister of Gujarat and is convinced of his business friendly policies.

The new government also needs to look at the two year long dispute between India and Italy arising from shooting of two Indian fishermen by Italian marines. With no quick resolution in sight, Italy has warned that the case may damage relations between the two countries.

But it must be said that after taking over as head of the government, the 63 year old Prime Minister who seems to be brimming with ideas, is giving out very little about his new governance model. The Prime Minister's Office is virtually impenetrable. His maiden speech in Parliament, a thanksgiving to the Presidential address, sought to convince members of Parliament that he means business and has in the past succeeded in delivering promises.

It is still early days in the PMO. To put an end to all the guessing game about the government's style of functioning, Mr Modi summed up in a blog his experience of the initial 30 days in office. The Prime Minister was quick to clarify that he did not have the luxury of extending the honeymoon period that previous governments enjoyed. At the same time, he assured the nation that in his first month in office, his "entire team has devoted every single moment for the welfare of the people" and "every decision we took was guided solely by national interest". While this may sound reassuring, one cannot ignore the remarks made by the Prime Minister about the Gujarat model in Parliament. The citizens of India who saw great promise in Mr Modi's Gujarat model of development may have been disappointed by the reality check they went through while hearing the Prime Minister's maiden impromptu speech in Parliament. Every voter who had the Gujarat model of development on his lips may have been taken aback when Mr Modi said that the much talked about Gujarat model of development cannot be replicated in another district of Gujarat. He said that Gujarat's second model is to learn from good examples set in any corner of the country.

His concern for the social sector was amply reflected in his speech in Parliament. So was his nationalist pride when he said, "The time has come to show our might to the world."

Mr Modi who takes great pride in his humble beginnings has begun attracting flattering comparisons to the late US President Richard Nixon and Japanese Prime Minister Shinzo Abe. Worthy of notice is the fact that he has 18 million friends on Facebook and is the second most popular politician in the world on Facebook. His style of governance that includes quick decision making and emphasis on punctuality, has galvanised Indian bureaucracy like never before. Keeping in mind the power of the social media, the Prime Minister has taken the welcome initiative of an online interactive mechanism that enables people to write to him directly.

That he is a go-getter and means business, is clear from the manner in which he has gone about going after black money stashed abroad within days of taking over.

Investment information and credit agency Icra gave Modi eight on a scale of 10 for his performace in the first month of holding the high office a month after taking oath on May 26.

In his aggressive campaign that the BJP described as "unprecedented in terms of outreach and innovation", Mr Modi's took care to address domestic priorities and touched upon key challenges before India. Beginning September 15, 2013, when he addressed his first rally after being appointed the BJP's PM candidate till May 10, 2014, when campaigning for the last phase ended, Narendra Modi addressed 440 rallies across India from Jammu to Kanyakumari, from Amreli to Arunachal Pradesh. The BJP claimed that from March 15 to May 10, he would have travelled almost 3 lakh kilometers! Apart from this, he held 1350 rallies held through the 3D technology across the nation.

And for his oath taking ceremony after an election that will be remembered for BJP's money power, Modi invited leaders of neighbouring countries. This unprecedented move by a head of government to invite leaders of SAARC countries to join his oath-taking function at the forecourt of Rashtrapati Bhawan, India's Presidential Palace, was not just symbolic. Putting behind years of acrimony and bitterness between India and Pakistan, Mr Modi reached out to Pakistan Prime Minister Nawaz Sharif who reciprocated by gracing the occasion. So did Nepal's Prime Minister, Sushil Koirala, Afghanistan President Hamid Karzai and many others. He chose Bhutan as his first overseas destination.

Mr Modi's speeches had an electrifying effect on people but it breathed life into the polls. The results were there for everybody to see. An otherwise disillusioned nation decided to exercise its franchise and the 2014 general elections earned the distinction of recording the highest voter turnout ever at 66.4 per cent.

The BJP argues that it inherited a bad growth rate of 4.8 per cent when it came to power under the leadership of Atal Behari Vajpayee in 1998. Yet when it demitted office in May 2004, it left a healthy growth rate of 8.5 per cent. The party says that inspite of so many global and domestic inhibiting factors, the BJP continued the growth story of India. It grappled with crisis triggered off by sanctions imposed on India following Pokhran II blasts, the Kargil war, the attack on Indian

Parliament, the East Asian crisis, the earthquake in Gujarat and the drought in 2002. From 2003 to 2008, India recorded an unprecedented nine per cent rate of growth but by the end of UPA II, the government led by Dr Singh was trying hard to revive the growth momentum.

The BJP may do well to assess with a balanced approach the policies of the previous regime and continue some good moves by the Congress such as the well intended Mahatma Gandhi National Rural Employment Guarantee Scheme that guarantees a minimum of 100 days employment, the emphasis on education in UPA II and the decision to raise a mountain strike corps along the China border with an aim to strengthen its military force along the LAC.

In the very first fortnight of taking charge, the Modi government was thrown into a difficult situation arising from the abduction of 40 construction workers, mostly from Punjab, in Mosul, Iraq, by the militant group ISIS. This was followed by 46 Indian 2014 the government made a major breakthrough with the nurses getting released. While efforts to secure the release of the 39 workers from Punjab are continuing, the government has gone out of its way to help all others returning on their own by providing some financial help/free air journey to those in need of the same.

The Modi government needs to identify the immediate pressing issues that are ailing the economy, address irritants in international relations, set the country in order by ensuring universal access to quality health care, provide much needed infrastructure and most importantly, create a safe and enabling environment for girls and women. Last but not the least, Mr Narendra Modi would do great service to the nation if he pursues the nation's economic interests and ensures a corruption free regime.

For a Prime Minister who grew with the the Rashtriya Swayam Sewak Sangh, the key challenge would be to keep his much admired governance free from the influences of the organisation. After all, the country has voted for good governance, freedom from corruption and long overdue development, not Hindutva.

10

Challenges in the Educational System for Narendra Modi

Sheetal Jain

Education lays the foundation of one's life.

Children begin learning while they're in the womb, and typically begin using their senses during the last trimester of a pregnancy. A child's body is formed from the mother's body; he goes through every emotion a mother is going through, and that's why mothers are advised to stay happy and think positively during their pregnancies. As is expected, children learn more after they are born from the people around them and through careful observation of their environments.

Their learning horizon expands exponentially when they enter into a formal school, where they meet different kinds of people, make friends and are formally taught. While earlier the learning was in an informal set up, now they learn in a planned and structured way, where their teachers teach them and present them with new thought processes to augment their learning.

Once they enter into a formal school most of the parents feel relieved because now their child's education is the school's responsibility. They hand over their child to a school for good 14-15 years and these are the most crucial years of anyone's life. These are the formative years that lay the foundation of what the children are going to become as individuals. A building is as strong as its foundation. If the foundation is strong, then the building can endure every change around it for a very long time; but if the foundation is weak, then the building might fall at anytime. Similarly, a strong education becomes the foundation of a successful life.

The Purpose of a Formal Education

The purpose of education is to prepare a child for their life in every way by inculcating life skills and preparing them for their career choices. That's why we always stress on the overall development of a child. An education system is complete only when it can provide overall growth to a child, i.e., physical, mental, emotional, social and spiritual.

However, while doing that we need to remember to help with the development of innate talent. Michelangelo, the master sculptor, was once asked how he was able to make sculptures from rocks. He responded by saying that all he did was set the sculpture free from the rock; *"I just remove what's not required."* In the same way, parents and teachers are the sculptors of a child's life. Each child is born with a unique ability and we need an education system that can enable a child with bringing out what best they are holding within. We are the ones who need to help each child with realizing their own potential so they can eventually become valuable assets for a nation's growth. With the right education an individual can contribute towards their growth as well as the growth of their country, especially when the collective impact of individual actions is calculated.

What Makes a New Generation Smarter?

The education system evolves and changes with every generation. Parents believe their children are always smarter than they were. When I was a five-year old, my mother said that she knew nothing in comparison to what I knew at that age. When I meet today's parents, they also have similar things to say. Every next generation is smarter than its previous generation and with good reason.

Each new generation learns from one that has gained significantly more experience. That being said, we must be extremely careful about what we say and do around our children because they imbibe that knowledge rapidly. For instance, my niece is 5-months old and she tries to copy what we say. She tries to move her lips in similar manner and speak. Although she cannot imitate or reproduce very complex words, her grasp of the smaller words is much higher. While this is a mild example, it's clear that if we had not evolved at this pace as humans, we still would have been living in the primitive age with stones as our tools.

And although evolution is good and necessary, it also needs to be coupled with a clear direction.

Gaps in the Education System: Why Do They Exist?

Because of my work, I meet many people and get to see their lives very closely. Often people talk about how there is a degradation of values in today's generation. But, I wondered how a child could be held responsible what is learned through our actions. As the source of learning we are responsible for what is happening in their environments. This thought took me to different schools to find out what had occurred to change the value system of today's children.

If you want to understand something, you need to get into the system to become a part of it. From the outside, you can only get a glimpse of how things are. So, when I joined the school again as a student, I had several discussions with parents, teachers and school principals. What I realized was we're all good human beings and we all have good intentions. However, we sometimes don't know how good we can be. We have many commitments and responsibilities, and we forget that as teachers we have a bigger responsibility to our students. Within their classrooms, teachers impact and shape up to 40 lives at a time. Once teachers realize this enormity, they can give much more compared to what they're giving now.

However, we can only give what we have. In other words, the values we are expecting from our children are the values we have been unable to impart. We might be teaching a certain set of values to them but if we have not been following them, our children will also not follow them. I cannot blame the teachers entirely. They are also humans and are on the receiving end of very real shortcomings in the system. Once during a motivational workshop for teachers in one school in Karnal Haryana, teachers expressed their concern regarding salaries paid to them. They shared that some teachers in school are paid as per the 6th pay commission and some are paid without following that norm. Because of lack of employment opportunities, they have accepted low salaries. However, the most painful part is they had not received salaries for last 6 months. In such a scenario, how can anyone expect them to be motivated to give their best to students and one teacher was very honest in accepting the fact that to manage his living he has to push children to take tuition from him. It was a shocking revelation which brought out a very big discrepancy in the education system. If we are not taking care of our educators, how can we expect them to stay motivated and give their best for our children?

Then the question was why they had agreed to work at lower salaries this is when I discovered a lack of preparedness and skills. I found out that although they had completed their professional training to work as teachers, in reality they might not have attended the proper course. They sought admission for their certification, bribed the coaching institutes and got their degrees. This took me to a further level of understanding of why the structure is not working and why there is a change in the value system. If teachers come with an aim to somehow obtain a degree by any means, they cannot teach ethics to small children.

We blame politicians and bureaucrats for corruption but have we thought about how and where it begins? It starts in schools. When a mother says, if you do your work I will give you a chocolate, she bribes her child. When a teacher thinks that she is in a job rather than considering that the responsibility of a child's life is on her, she has taught a child how to evade his responsibilities. When the school administration concentrates on filling up classes with students instead of improving teaching standards, they have taught a child unethical ways of living.

When a school does not pay salaries to its teachers it has shown very clearly that the educators are not valued. The more I explored the more scared I was. It looked like the system was crumbling at all levels. We might have advanced technologically, we might be providing smart classes and a very advanced curriculum, but until the thought process with which we are teaching is not corrected, it cannot bring the change that we desire.

Now, the bigger problem that I could see was that even teachers and parents are unaware of the damage because they have not been educated differently. If they aren't educated on the same values, how could they provide that to the future generation? The easiest "solution" to this problem is to sit and talk about what's wrong which allows us to shift our responsibility to someone else. But the truth is that every citizen of this country has a responsibility to work for the nation. It is very easy to point out what is bad, how people have become selfish, how corruption has increased, how women are unsafe and nothing has been done. The more we talk without doing, the more we add to what we do not want around us. We want a nation of love, peace and harmony but all we talk about is how bad things are.

And what I feel is simply this:

> *We cannot create a nation of love, peace and harmony by focusing on the eradication of crime. We need to focus on creating love, peace and harmony.*

Changing the Thought Process

If you want to deal with corruption, you cannot just tell a child not to take bribe; you need to teach a child to be honest. If you do not want people to fight, you cannot just tell them not to fight; instead, show them how to love. If you do not want people to lie, you cannot just tell them not to lie. You need to teach them how to speak the truth. We need to talk about all the good we can bring and how it can be done.

Once I got an opportunity to be with a few educators who were talking about how this whole system should be. They were all over 60 years old and had spent more than 30 to 40 years in the education system. They all had retired from senior administrative posts like Principals, Vice Chancellors or Heads of the Departments at their universities. While sitting among them I realized that they wanted to bring good things, but in their own way. They wanted to bring in old thoughts they were connected to rather than thinking of new solutions. They were attached to how they had seen things, ignoring what was happening in front of them. They are far from what the youth of today want. They talk about limiting the use of mobile phones and tablets or computers in school but they forget the fact that can't be expected to use outdated technologies either. As a race, we have written on stones, then on leaves, on slates, paper and now on computers. That is how we have evolved and we cannot resist change. If we want to reach the hearts of the youth, we need to teach them with methods they grasp instead of forcing them to follow what we believe to be right. We want young children to learn our ways but we are not ready to learn their ways. This one way thought process can never work even if we have the best of intentions in our hearts. We cannot force change on someone and if we do, we take away his or her power to think and act in a natural way. That is why we see schools and other institutions of learning churn out legions of followers instead of leaders and change-agents. We tell our children stories of famous people and we ask them to follow in their footsteps. When you teach your children to be followers, how can you expect them to lead?

These educators also talked about the many reports and commissions formed to suggest changes in the education system since Independence. However, either the implementation has been much delayed or many suggestions have not been implemented up till now. For example Common School System was suggested by Kothari Commission on Education in 1964-66 and was also supported in National Policy of Education in 1986 and 1992 has yet to be implemented. Even after 50 years of its recommendation millions of children attend ill maintained government schools and are taught by unmotivated teachers. These children rarely dream of getting into main stream of education and getting good jobs. Clearly, setting up a commission and making a report does not ensure the advent of change. The big question is what can bring change? How can we implement the things we want and need?

Why is the Old System Failing?

Because I had already heard that so many reports were made and so many proposals had been sent, I decided to see what I could do. When I attended school again, I realized that the ego was increasing in every individual because of a lack of gratitude. We have stopped caring for others because there is a lack of compassion. We have diseases because there is a lack of training on health. We talk about the reservation system and we want our children to treat everyone equally, which is not possible.

So we cannot talk young children into letting go of their ego. We need to bring in more love in their lives and in the ways we educate them. We need to be compassionate ourselves and train our young generation to be compassionate. All this cannot happen with implementing some project; it has to be imbibed in our day-to-day life. Limiting this change to assignments and projects does not work, especially because parents/tutors complete most of the projects and assignments. Parents are more focused on their child getting the best grade in the class rather than looking at the purpose of the assignment and what their child would learn from it. For them, a special project means extra work. So, obviously, limiting the training to projects and assignments doesn't work. A change needs to be brought into day-to-day life and for that we need to train parents and teachers.

There are three stakeholders' in a child's life: the parents, the teachers and the child. The old education system focuses only on training a child but the child learns from teachers and parents; if the influencers have not been trained properly, the child's education remains incomplete and consequently, what's taught in school does not take root in a child's mind. When he comes back home, he steps into an entirely different world because a gap exists between the two.

The child starts disconnecting from people around him and that is how children build a new world of their own. If we want to penetrate into their world, we need to bring harmony into their lives. We can't just hand them a pre-set thought process; we need to educate them on how to think. Once I was talking about morality with small children and I asked them how they could become good human beings. They wrote a few points and the most common answer was by helping others, which is a good idea. But, when I asked them how they could help others, no one had any answer. After 30 minutes of brainstorming and discussion, they could make points on how we could help. We want children to think in a positive direction but we have not trained them on how to think in a positive manner. When I asked these children to write about their school, their teachers and themselves, they could; but when I specifically asked them to write 5 positive points of each, they could not.

It's quite evident that we need to train young minds on how to think in the right direction instead of giving them a set thought process. In the old system, teachers have been teaching in a set pattern and they resist change. I have seen teachers saying, 'believe it because I say so!' If this is how we are teaching, then we can never reach where we want to reach. As teachers it is our prime responsibility to understand the child we are dealing with. We also need to understand what type of personality the child has. We need to listen patiently to what they are saying and then relate our ideas with their ideas rather than insisting a forced acceptance.

Every parent wants their child to be the best. However they don't always know what the best is. To make their child the best, they enter into a blind race that has no end. When I asked parents what type of school they wanted for their child, everyone had a common answer: they wanted the best school. When I asked what the best was according to them, they did not have an immediate answer. When asked what the "best" comprised, they were unable to give anything but vague answers. They wanted the best but they did not know what was best and the small child had to fulfill their ambition.

Parents enroll their child to different hobby classes without realizing whether their child is able to connect with that activity or not. If children were kept busy with various activities throughout the day, when would their minds find time to develop their own thought process?

Without having developed a unique thought process, children are unable to develop leadership skills, creative thinking skills or even analytical skills. And without time for personal creative expression, they can start developing an anguish inside which can manifest as resentment towards society, school and parents.

Critical Research Observations

Regardless of the reason behind it, I accept that there is a change in the attitude of younger children, along with changes in the attitudes of parents and teachers as well but they are not always positive.

The Students

> *Today's generation is an entitled generation and they feel they have a right to demand everything they want. Common attitudes that I had observed were:*

1. I deserve everything.
2. If "it" is done for everyone, then why not for me.
3. More should be done for me.
4. Why should I take initiative?
5. Why should I be thankful?
6. I am special and different (True but we cannot ignore the fact that everyone else is special and different too).
7. I should have an upper hand.
8. I should get my rights.
9. I do not need self-evaluation.
10. I am better than others and I should be proved better than others.
11. More focus on external looks and rewards.
12. Short-term goal realization to satisfy the ego.
13. Running in a rat race to prove something.

15. I should make others pay for their mistakes.
16. I am insecure about my image (Makes a person depends on others approval).
17. I am insecure about my rights (Makes a person greedy and hoard more than he needs).
18. Like to work less and demand more.
19. Want others to do things for them.
20. Feels great by others as lesser.

The Parents

1. My child should get the best.
2. No one should find fault with my child.
3. My child cannot be wrong.
4. My child should get special attention.
5. The school is responsible for everything.
6. I can spend money and can buy anything for my child.
7. A focus on grades and book learning as opposed to the overall learning and growth of the child.

The Teachers

1. Teaching is my job, not my responsibility.
2. I already know all, no one can teach me anything new.
3. Schools are not doing enough for us.
4. Kids have a habit of arguing and troubling us, so they need to be suppressed.
5. Many chose teaching as a profession because they did not find themselves suitable for any other profession.
6. More focus on completing the course rather than what the child is learning. Though a new Continuous and Comprehensive Evaluation (CCE) system has been designed and teachers are supposed to evaluate students as per that but most of the teachers are good at completing the records and following the old ways.

7. Still adopting the old ways of punishment, which only cultivate fear in children. However, the purpose of punishment fails when the child repeats the same mistakes. There is no self-realization.

I am not judging these attitudes as right or wrong because these are what have been learned and implemented. I am not saying that old system was wrong but it needs to be revived with new means. We need to keep the old and new together, so that all the generations can walk together. By understanding all these factors I realized that we need an overhauling of the education system, which not only deals in giving a new way of educating young minds but also can give a new mindset to the teachers and parents too.

A System Overhaul: The Need of the Hour

It is very difficult to repair an old building but it is easier to make a new building. Similarly, it is difficult to repair the entire old system completely, but it would be easier to make a new education system, which is designed the way we want to see our nation.

To design an education system, first we need to have a vision for the education system and then design it accordingly. Once we have the vision, we need to make a blueprint of the system. Now, the purpose of education is not to educate; it is a means to achieve the vision. This means needs to be in alignment with the vision, which we have for our nation, because education lays the foundation of the citizens of a country. So, if we want to see India as a loving, peaceful and progressive country, we need to design our education system with a vision to create loving, peaceful and progressive citizens. The big question is whether the current education system has the provisions for the fulfillment of these goals. The course material, books, workshops, schools, teachers' training programmes, education institutes for teachers, parents education programmes and higher education programmes, colleges, universities, and professional courses all have to be designed as per the vision. We need to make a blueprint of what the schools should look like, how the teachers should be and how we need to train the parents. We also need to fill the gap in teachers' training so that they can begin approaching their profession with dedication.

Reforms Required in the Education System

We need to bring in reform at all levels.

1. Redesign Government Schools

In India, more than 70 per cent of the schools are fully or partially funded by the government. Children studying in these schools do not get admitted easily to good colleges. A person belonging to middle class or above would not like to send their child to the government school though they are funded by the tax paid by them. Families living below the poverty line (BPL) send their children to government schools, but often times they don't have the proper access to their education.

Parents of such children have very little interest in education. They are busier in making their ends meet rather than focusing on their child's upbringing. If the child is old enough to do a little work, they make them work instead of study. So, we need to appoint volunteers and train them to visit such houses in villages and slums. These volunteers can make sure that the child comes to school. Also, we need to bring the quality of education in government schools at par with the private schools. Eliminating private schools is not an option, but we need to provide quality education in government schools, so that there is no difference between the child who has studied from a government school and the child who has studied from private school.

The same principle must be applicable for colleges too. We need to elevate the standard of education in colleges or let us say every institute that is funded by the government. The Indian government is the largest provider of education in India but the quality of education is far behind than what we would want to see. To improve the quality of education, we will need more resources. Though these colleges have been receiving sufficient aid, to generate more funds, a nominal fee can be charged from the students. Additionally, students need to be involved in the maintenance of the school, so that they can also realize their responsibility. It is very easy to not value or respect a service offered for free. But when we are involved in its day-to-day maintenance, the direct consequence is an increase in the level of responsibility. The tasks can be divided as per the age and how much load the child can take.

More accountability and discipline should be added in government institutes rather than giving them a free hand and the "security for life" mindset that comes with a governmental position must be eliminated. Every teacher should be made accountable depending on the performance the students.

2. Reform in Teachers' Training

A 6-month or 1-year course cannot create a teacher. When we need 3+2 years for engineering, management, medicine, and computers or for other professional courses, why do we allot just few months for teacher certifications? It means we have not treated the teaching profession seriously. First of all, we need to bring the teaching profession into the mainstream and we need to design a full-fledged 3-year graduation course and 2-year post-graduation course to become an eligible teacher. As a result, the teacher who graduates from such colleges has high self-esteem and is motivated to implement what has been learned instead of perpetuating the self-defeating cycle of not being able to find other gainful employment.

And instead of relying on a trial-and-error method, there should be a high level of scrutiny in a teacher's selection process. Along with the degree, we also need to evaluate a teacher's attitude towards children and how responsible the teacher tends to be. We also need to train teachers with understanding child psychology. Studying child psychology and general psychology should be mandatory for all teachers to enable their understanding of children for their growth and strength-development.

It is a teacher's responsibility to find out a child's passion and strengths and then motivate child towards it. However, this task needs the right training to be executed with any success.

3. Education Programmes for Parents

Schools need to introduce special education programmes for parents to help them approach their child's education in a productive and holistic manner. The first time, parents should be taught on how to be a good parent, as they may not have the experience in parenting; it's quite common to see parents displace their frustration on their children and bring up their child the way they were brought up. They do not realize that with changing times, their child's needs are also changing. Special workshops about handling the very real issues their kids face should be organized in schools, so that parents can also learn and evolve and understand their children in a better way.

4. Redesign the Course Curriculum

We need to design a curriculum, which can focus on the overall development of a child, which includes their spiritual and psychological development. When a child grows up, he is aware of his presence, his strengths and is not worried about the competition. We need to prepare a curriculum, which can bring children on the path of love and equality, where the child understands that the difference in work and income does not make people better or lesser than each other; where the child also learns that a difference in gender, region or religion does not have to be divisive. If we want to eliminate all the differences, we need to teach equality. For that we need to retrain our teachers so that they can also operate with equality at the forefront.

Along with redesigning, special arrangements in the government schools and colleges can be made where we can show the lectures from reputed institutes. There can be a live telecast from good colleges and institutes or their recorded sessions can be broadcasted.

Also, a curriculum needs to be designed which can inculcate self-motivation in a child towards personal development and the development of the nation. Again, specialized training for teachers is required for the fulfillment of this objective.

5. Redesign the Examination System

Why do we need exams? When we have taken a child in school/college/institute shouldn't it be our responsibility to train him? Why do we have to give grades to students? If a child has taken admission in engineering, tight scrutiny should be held at that time rather than when he is passing out. We should have so much faith in our education that we do not need to grade our students. If the child has to learn as per his capability, then why did we take a child in a course for which he was not capable enough? Was our focus only on admission at that time? Instead of focusing on exams, our focus should be on what the child is learning. If a computer engineer is unable to differentiate between hardware and software, it proves that he did not learn about computers; he only completed his degree! So, instead of designing an exit examination, we need to design an entry examination and once we have accepted the child in the system, it is our responsibility to make sure he learns. While taking admission in the next level education, again the child must go through a test rather than demonstrating a purely grade-based progress report.

6. Create More Jobs

There is a dearth of jobs for the youth who has not taken a professional degree. More jobs should be created like in manufacturing sector, construction sectors etc. which require further investment from the government, which can be achieved only with good governance which we are expecting with the change in government.

The education system is the backbone of any country and it's the perfect environment to inculcate new ideologies. Today we need to create well-rounded and responsible citizens first instead of creating doctors or engineers. If an individual is a doctor or a teacher and is not a good human being, they will not be able to deliver what has pledged and then will likely resort to malpractice.

We need to create an education system which can cultivate love, equality and peace and for that we need to bring reform at all levels the way we have been teaching, what we've taught and the people who are teaching. If we want to change India, we need to change its education system.

We are hoping for better governance with the change in government and that should bring the much-awaited change.

Education today needs to be organized holistically. It is not only the 3Rs—reading, writing, and arithmetic—which should be well-taught but should cover alongside many other aspects, for example practical guidance on how to live a good and healthy life.

Education must effectively cover aspects like:

- Personal Hygiene
- Public Hygiene
- Sense of right and wrong
- Social adjustability/tolerance
- Moral courage/moral values
- Nationalism/national pride
- Human rights and obligations

Why does it take six decades for consciousness to be raised about a very important function of life like defecating which has unfortunately, for too long, been accepted as an act which can be or is done in the open? The 'open' in the countryside is the countryside itself. In cities and towns, those who do not have toilets in their houses resort to relieving themselves outside their own dwelling on the streets. Why has it taken India that long to raise consciousness about such undesirable/unhealthy/unhygienic modes of defecating? It is high time that this important aspect of toilet training is covered thoroughly in schools.

Another aspect, which must be well provided for in education, is the inculcation of nationalism, national pride and related matters, because children have very little connections with the stories of people who have accomplished great deeds for their fellow citizens. C History—correct history and not any doctored version—must be taught, so that it is we learn from it and do not repeat mistakes of the past which will endanger a adversely affect our future.

There's an old African proverb, which says, "It takes a village to raise a child." Without a doubt, raising our children into successful and well-developed citizens requires pouring in a lot of effort and attention by many different sections of society; but if we want our nation to flourish and stand proudly alongside all the developed countries in the world, fixing the education system will be an investment we will have to make.

11

Good Governance in India:
The Imperatives of Human Rights-Based Development Approach

Suresh R

Introduction

The term good governance implies the effective management of a nation's resources in a manner that is open, transparent, accountable, equitable and responsive to people's needs. Therefore, the rule of law, transparency, accountability and effectiveness of public sector management and an active civil society are all essential components of good governance. It appears that good governance is closely related to the system of government. The democratic system has been considered as the best form of government for good governance, as it aspire for the welfare of all and strive to solve problems amicably through deliberations.

When we examine the issues related to good governance in India it is important to see the governance system prevalent in the immediate past. India was under the colonial rule for about two hundred years before becoming independent in mid-20th century. This had an impact on the present governance system in India. The colonial power had established the administrative system in British India to cater their requirements. The concerns of native population were reflected neither in their policies nor in their administration. Most of these administrative practices are still following in the governance of India without major change.

Though India has adopted a democratic system of government which functions on the principle of consent of the people, the administrative system in India is not responsive to the peoples demand or aspirations. This is mainly because of the dichotomy between local needs and administrative system which has been formed for entirely different purpose. The British administrative system was established to cater the British colonial interests. The advent of Independence and adoption of a democratic system of governance demanded a new set of institutions and administration. The key areas of administrations such as district administration, police administration and educational administration are clear examples of colonial influence. Even after six decades of Independence no major changes are effected in the administrative system. The British pattern of district administration with district collector holding all administrative power is still practiced in India. Similarly, the one and a half century-old 1861 Police Act still forms the basic code for maintaining law and order in India. Again, the Official Secrets Act of 1923 is still practiced, which permits the officials to keep most of the official transaction as secret and common people have no access to these documents.[1] A minor amendment to this was effected with the Right to Information (RTI) Act of 2005; till then for nearly for fifty-seven years after Independence India's democratic system was carrying the colonial Act without any change. Further some of the draconian laws such as AFSPA (Armed Forces Special Powers Act) is in force in the North East and Jammu and Kashmir.[2] The prevalence of such Acts and legislations which are in contravention to fundamental human rights guaranteed in part III and also against the democratic principles are still enshrined in the constitution of India.

In the educational field we still practice the colonial method of creating different layers in the society. Those who have access to learn the elite language of English have a better position in administration and governance than their less fortunate counterparts who study in their native language. This anomaly in the educational system is well reflected in the higher bureaucracy of India. Though there are provisions for reservation of posts in government services including higher bureaucracy the representation of backward classes, scheduled castes and scheduled tribes are not in proportion to their population even after sixty-seven years of Independence.

Again, the rural development programmes and strategies are initiated and implemented by the bureaucracy that has little knowledge about the local requirements of the rural people settled in various regions. The beneficiaries of any rural development programme except the Mahatma Gandhi National Rural Employment Guarantee Programme (MNREGP) are identified and implemented by the bureaucrats. Though the 73 and 74 Constitution Amendment Acts[3] proposes democratic decentralisation, in actual practice, the *Panchayati Raj* institutions are functioning without adequate resources or administrative mandate. In tune with the colonial administration the district collector wield all administrative power in the district administration. The administrative machinery is entangled with rules and procedures and it is neither effective nor efficient to find solution to the problem confronted by common man in their daily life.

The official statistics of the government of India shows that the economy has grown at an average annual rate of about 6 per cent for the last five years. However, the gap between rich and the poor is widening at an alarming rate. India's recent economic growth has been attributed to the service industry, but 60 per cent of the workforce remains in agriculture. The small farmers are still entangled in debt trap and forced to commit suicide.[4] It shows that the benefits of ongoing economic reforms process is not reaching the rural area where the majority of the population struggle to earn a livelihood. The economic disparity between the haves and have-nots is further aggravated with social inequality prevalent in the Indian society.

Though formally the caste system has been abolished in India, informally it is practiced in the society. In the prevailing social hierarchy in India, the lower castes are treated inferior. The slow pace of social mobility in the social system shows that caste determines one's social status in the society. It appears that the effects of caste system and the practice of apartheid policy are same. The prevalence of apartheid-like caste system and economic inequality in India also adversely affect good governance.

Those who are socially and economically deprived cannot expect good governance. They further land up in a vicious circle from which they cannot come out. The social inequality augments poverty and this in turn leads to illiteracy and unemployment. Therefore, under the prevailing socio-economic inequality condition those who are backward and poor cannot come out of this vicious circle. This again points towards the denial of human rights to those who are born in socially and economically backward families. Low family socio-economic level and low level of education are examples of social determinants that negatively influence good governance. It appears that the human right-based development approach would help to address the problems of socio-economic inequality and bring good governance in India.

Bureaucracy and Economic Development in India

According to Fred W. Riggs bureaucracy and economic development are intimately interdependent.[5] Similar views were expressed by a number of social scientists.[6] An effective and efficient bureaucratic structure is *sine quo non* for progress, especially in developing countries. Therefore, effective and efficient bureaucracy has been considered an important agency to promote and sustain the development process. However, a close look in the actual functioning of bureaucracy in India shows that it fails to incorporate the ideals for which it was established.

Indira Gandhi, the former Prime Minister of India disgustingly referred to the administrative machinery as 'the stumbling block in the country's progress' and reiterated the necessity of creating an administrative cadre committed to national objectives and responsive to Indian social needs. She found in 'committed bureaucracy' the answer to the ills of Max Weber's[7] concept of bureaucratic neutrality that crippled the development process in India because of lack of commitment. She had an earnest belief that only a committed bureaucracy can bring about the desired change in the country.

However, the committed bureaucracy created another major problem as observed by the Vohra Committee Report of 1993, which was set up to look into the criminalisation of politics.[8] The report observed that the mafia and the criminals enjoyed the patronage of politicians and the protection of government functionaries. It pointed out how the nexus was virtually running a parallel government, pushing the state apparatus into irrelevance. The illicit nexus between bureaucracy and political executive poses another major threat to good governance in India.

Too many rules and procedures not only lead to corruptions but also people losing faith in the administration. The former Prime Minister of India, Rajiv Gandhi himself admitted that the administrative cost for implementing People Welfare Programme is seventy 5 per cent of the actual allocations. That means if rupees 100 is to reach a beneficiary by means of subsidy or other welfare fund rupees 75 would be spent as administrative cost and the actual beneficiary would get rupees 25 after a prolonged delay. Thus most of the welfare programmes aimed at poverty alleviation are not reaching the actual beneficiaries.

The higher bureaucracy in India is trained mainly to maintain records and follow procedures in the administrative system which were developed and practiced during the colonial rule. They are not exposed to the real ground situations. Most of them come from urban elite family background. They are not aware of the problems of 70 per cent of the population who dwells in rural areas. Therefore, it is not surprising that they are indifferent to the aspirations of the rural people. The bureaucrats treat the ordinary people as their subjects who live at their mercy. The concept of civil servants as the servants of the people is yet to emerge in the Indian administrative system. This again adversely affects the prospects of good governance.

The indifferent attitude of bureaucracy towards the people is visible not only at the higher bureaucratic levels but also at the middle and lower levels. The problems of the people were addressed not from individual case-by-case basis but by age-old colonial system-based rules and procedures. Those who approach the government departments for various purposes were treated with suspicion. This again is rooted in the administrative system during the colonial rule. The mistrust which prevails between the civil servants and the ordinary people is a major problem for good governance in India.

The age-old Colonial Acts, rules and procedures need to be changed at the earliest. Minor changes or half hearted attempt towards such changes have little impact. Any move towards good governance has to incorporate measures to sensitise the bureaucracy to address the people's problem in a friendly and positive manner. A genuine democratic decentralisation is to be effected to do so.

In a democratic system delay in taking decisions add to the problem of effective and efficient administration. The state service delivery is an important component of development strategies. However, the present service delivery in India is not up to the expectation of the people. That is why India is still confronted with the same problem such as poverty, illiteracy and unemployment, even after the implementation of eleven five-year plans since Independence. One of the focal point of all five-year plans since Independence has been eradication of poverty. However, even after sixty-four years of planned economic development programmes framed and implemented through a colonial model of bureaucracy, nearly one-third of the population still remain below poverty line. Therefore, one of the options is to initiate a rights-based development approach, because, under this approach situation analysis is used to identify immediate, underlying and basic causes of development problems. Again, in this approach people are recognised as key actors in their own development, rather than passive recipients of commodities and services, and participation of people is considered as both a means and a goal.

The 'compulsions of coalition government' and lack of an able political leadership with providence too adversely affect good governance in India. The existence of draconian laws such as Armed Forces (Special Powers) Act (AFSPA), a reminiscence of the colonial days, is still prevalent in some parts of India. The judiciary which acts as the custodian of fundamental rights of the citizen is overloaded with pending cases which leads to delay in delivery of justice. Thus, the institutional mechanisms established under the democratic system in Independent India are not properly functioning to satisfy the aspirations of the poor people who constitute a major portion of the population.

Good Governance in India and Economic Inequality

The official statistics of the government of India shows that the economy has grown at an average annual rate of about 6 per cent for the last five years, reducing poverty by 10 per cent. However, 40 per cent of the world's poor still live in India, and 27 per cent of the country's population continues to live below the poverty line. More than one-third live on less than a dollar a day, and 80 per cent live on less than two dollars a day. India's recent economic growth has been attributed to the service industry, but 60 per cent of the workforce remains in agriculture.[9]

The disparity between the 'haves' and the 'have-nots' is increasing at an alarming rate. Urban elites in technology-related professions are accumulating wealth and living in luxury. The cities are growing in all directions and farmlands are being acquired to build luxury townships, golf courses and five star hotels and clubs. The poor farmers get paid off and are forced to move further away from the town where there are no infrastructural facilities like water supply, transport and electricity. While on the one side India is growing as an IT superpower, on the other side everyone turns a blind eye to the majority of the population who live in rural area, untouched by the economic growth.

It is quite obvious that India's recent economic growth has not trickled down to the bottom. For the poor, lack of basic health, education and skill development mean that not only are they in a miserable condition today, there is not much hope for the future either. The official statistics below further support this statement.

1. 27.5 per cent of Indians live below the national income poverty line.
2. More than 60 per cent of women are chronically poor, as are 43 per cent of Scheduled Tribes and 36 per cent of Scheduled Caste groups.

3. More than 90 per cent of the overall workforce is employed in the informal economy; 96 per cent of women are in the informal economy.
4. 48.6 per cent of farmer households are in debt, and only 27 per cent have access to formal credit.
5. 296 million people are illiterate and 233 million are undernourished.
6. 254 per 100,000 live births is the maternal mortality rate and is an indicator not only of the quality of maternal health care services but also of the level of empowerment of women.[10]

The basic question is can a country where one-third of the population are illiterate and living below poverty line be expecting good governance? While India's educated elite are revealing in their new found status on the global stage, inequitable distribution of wealth and opportunities are shaking the very foundation of India's economy. The prevailing economic inequality therefore has an adverse impact on good governance in India.

The governmental structures have so far contented themselves by chalking out only strategies for promotion of economic and social rights since Independence. Those strategies have hardly borne any fruits because of rampant corruption at the political executive as well as permanent executive levels. The UN estimate shows that millions of people in India live in a state of abject poverty, without food, shelter, employment, health care and education. According to UNDP Report of 2010, Indian society is a highly inequitable society where the richest 10 per cent consume 33.5 per cent of resources and the poorest 10 per cent get only 3.5 per cent of resources. Around 233 million people are chronically hungry. Around 51 per cent of the population does not have sustainable access to affordable essential drugs. Infant mortality rate is 68 per 1000; child mortality rate under the age of 5 is 93 per 1000; 26 per cent children are underweight and 24 per cent of the population is undernourished. The maternal mortality ratio is 440 per 1,00,000 and 72 per cent of the population does not have access to improved sanitation.[11]

It is the prevailing grave economic inequality which leads to the identification of three India by the Department for International Development (DFID) in Britain: global India, developing India and poorest India.[12] Global India is the India of the new service industries, a growing industrial sector and large farmers. Global India is prosperous, linked to the global economy and reaping the benefits of globalisation. Developing India is the India of small farmers, micro-enterprises and village industries, which have some links to the modern economy, but have low productivity and limited access to public services. Poorest India is the India of the marginal farmer, landless agricultural labourers and urban slum dwellers, where people live in extreme poverty and basic public services are mostly absent.[13]

The Indian Parliament adopted 86th Constitutional Amendment whereby elementary education has been made fundamental right in the Constitution.[14] Despite this Amendment around 35 per cent of the population is still illiterate. About 50 million children are out of school. Even where enrolment is high, the dropout rate is over 50 per cent by the time the students move over to high school. Gender Parity Index is 0.82. It means for every 1000 boys enrolled, there are 820 girls seeking admissions. Can a country with such an unequal distribution of opportunities and wealth ever promise good governance?

Good Governance in India and Social Inequality

India was the first country in 1946 to raise its voice against apartheid at the UN and played a leading role towards its abolition. The Indian Constitution prohibits discrimination on grounds of religion, race, caste, sex or place of birth and affirms the right to equality, including equality before law and equality of opportunity in matters of employment as fundamental rights. The Indian Criminal Code and the Indian Penal Code contain provisions which prohibit racial discrimination and dissemination of ideas which promote disharmony on various grounds including race.

In the international arena India played an active part in the drafting of the International Convention on the Elimination of all forms of Racial Discrimination and was among its early signatories. India considers that besides theories of racial superiority, that are a legacy of the colonial period, the other sources and causes of racism and racial discrimination must be addressed. These include glaring economic disparities among various parts of the world which sustain and strengthen racist attitudes; the onslaught of bigotry, chauvinism and violence on diversity, pluralism and tolerance; absence of democracy, constitutional order and rule of law; political concept in which foreigners are regarded as rivals or competitors and a threat to local prosperity, culture and identity; immigration, citizenship and refugee laws with racist overtones and political platforms such as neo-Nazism that are based on race-related hatred and discrimination. India also voices its concern on the policies of oppression of national, sectarian and linguistic minorities.

Caste System in India—Is it apartheid?

Even though India championed the cause of apartheid in all international forums apartheid-like social stigma and caste system are still prevalent in India. This appears to be one of the reasons that recently the officials of the Ministry of External Affairs strongly rejected the opinion of Prime Minister Manmohan Singh that there is similarity between apartheid and caste system in India. Though there is much similarity between these two, the acceptance of this proposition would put India in a very embarrassing situation in international forums. That is the reason behind the fact that India is against equating apartheid with caste system in international forums.[15] The Indian delegation appeared before the UN human rights forum and refused to share data on the steps taken to end caste system in India. Instead, it argued that descent-based discrimination does not constitute racial discrimination under the specific UN treaty, the Convention on the Elimination of Racial Discrimination. It was India that suggested the definition in the Convention on Elimination of Racial Discrimination be expanded for descent-based discrimination to include caste when the treaty was being drafted. India's current position simply disavows its own past stand on the subject.

Though formally the caste system has been abolished in India, informally it is practiced in the Indian society. In the prevailing social hierarchy, the lower castes are treated inferior. The slow pace of social mobility in the Indian social system shows that caste determines one's social status in the society. The effects of caste system and the practice of apartheid policy are same. The only difference is that while apartheid policy had the official support, caste system has only the informal or societal support. Thus, with regard to the effects of caste system in Indian society and the apartheid or racial discrimination practiced by the Whites in South Africa, there is much similarity between these two social evils. The existing caste system in the Indian society appears to be one of the causes for low profile involvement of India on the human rights issues in international forums. In this context it is interesting to note that the Chairman of the Drafting Committee of the Indian Constitution B.R. Ambedkar had rightly observed on the eve of the introduction of the new constitution of India that "on the 26th January, 1950 we are going to enter into a life of contradictions. In politics we will have equality and in social and economic life we will have inequality". The prevalence of apartheid-like caste system and economic inequality in India also adversely affect good governance. It appears that the problem of prevailing socio-economic inequality can be better addressed through human rights-based development approach.

Human Rights-Based Development Approach Towards Good Governance

The human rights-based development approach offers the possibility for progressive interventions of the state into the social economic inequality in three ways: First, International Convention on the Elimination of all forms of Racial Discrimination signed by most countries in the world and thus can be considered to embody **universal values** and aspirations. Second, human rights conventions place a legal obligation upon states. This view was endorsed by Mary Robinson, the former UN High Commissioner for Human Rights. She said "...a human rights approach adds value because it provides a normative framework of obligations that has the legal power to render governments **accountable**".[16] Third, human rights-based language can help to **direct policy**. It shifts the focus of debate from the personal failures of the "poor" to the failure of macro-economic structures and policies implemented by nation-states and international bodies (World Trade Organisation, World Bank, International Monetary Fund, etc.) to eradicate poverty. Hence, poverty in this context is no longer described as a "social problem" but a "**violation of rights**".[17]

The rights-based approach also helps to address the problem of socio-economic inequality and absence of good governance in India. Those who are socially and economically deprived cannot expect good governance. They further landed up in a vicious circle from which they cannot come out easily. The social inequality augments poverty and this in turn leads to illiteracy and illiteracy leads to unemployment. This is well reflected when one examines the unfilled vacancies reserved for backward classes and scheduled castes for the want of qualified candidates. Therefore, under the prevailing socio-economic inequality condition those who are backward and poor cannot come out of this vicious circle. This again point towards the denial of human rights to those who are born in socially and economically backward class family. Low family socio-economic level and low level of education are examples of social determinants that negatively influence good governance. The programme initiated under inclusive growth appears to be based on the human rights-based approach towards development.

Again, the IT-enabled e-governance makes the administrative system more transparent, accountable and effective. The legislative measures such as Right to Information Act and Citizen Charter, Right to Public service Right to Food etc.[18] are some initiative towards reforms in administrative system towards good governance. Another positive trend in this area is the role of civil society organisations in the governance of the country is being increasingly visible and acceptable.

However, minor changes and reforms in certain areas are not enough to realise good governance. What is needed is a major change in the administrative system and governance. However, the Indian bureaucracy, especially the higher bureaucracy is grown very powerful to nip in the bud any reforms initiated by the political executive. The weak political executive always travels through the beaten track shown by the permanent executive as that path is easier and less risky. The 'compulsions of coalition' and lack of a long-term perspective along with bureaucratic inefficiency adversely affect India's move towards good governance. The existence of social and economic inequality appears to have further aggravated the problem of good governance. In such a situation the human rights-based development approach[19] appears to be the best means towards good governance. For all programmes under this approach focus on marginalised, disadvantaged and excluded groups. Moreover, this approach also envisages the participation of the people both a means and end.

NOTES AND REFERENCES

1. The Official Secrets Act 1923 enacted on 2 April 1923 during the British period is nearly ninety-one years old. Available at: www.*india.gov.in/allimpfrms/allacts/3314.pdf* Accessed on 12/12/2011
2. AFSPA is in force in most of the North Eastern States and Jammu & Kashmir. This act empowers the armed forces to arrest and conduct search and even kill people who are suspects for anti-national activist in view of the armed forces officers. Though there is worldwide protest by the human right activist against this inhuman law the government is not ready to repeal this act mainly because of compulsion from security forces. In all international forums concerned with human rights protection and promotion India was criticised for the enforcement of such anti-democratic laws.
3. The Indian Constitution 73rd Amendment Act, 1992 came into effect from 24th April 1993. The revitalisation of Panchayati Raj manifested through the 73rd Constitutional Amendment owes its origin to Prime Minister Rajiv Gandhi. He said that "If our district administration is not sufficiently responsive, the basic reason is that it is not only sufficiently representative. With the decay of Panchayati Raj Institutions, the administration has got isolated from the people thus dulling its sensitivity to the needs of the people". With 73rd & 74th Amendment Acts it was expected that PRIs that have come up under the Acts would be devolved of functions, finances and the functionaries to enable them to emerge as institutions of self-government. The PRIs are expected to play a multifaceted role. They are vehicles for political education and training in leadership. They have to be responsive to the needs of the community, impart values of equality and liberty, be transparent, accountable and efficient and to provide opportunities for mass participation in the process of development. Report of the Working Group on Decentralised Planning & Panchayati Raj Institutions Available at: *www.planningcommission.nic.in/aboutus/committee/wrkgrp/wg_decn.pdf.* Accessed on 12/12/2011.
4. *The Hindu*, dated 20 March 2014.
5. Fred W. Riggs, Administration in Developing Countries, 1964, pp. 243-259.
6. Ferrel Heady, for instance, believes that a highly efficient well-organised and effective bureaucracy is first necessity for development in developing countries. Report of

Personnel Administration, Administrative Reforms Commission, Govt. of India, 1969, p. 1.

7. Max Weber's bureaucracy is characterized by hierarchical organisation, delineated lines of authority in a fixed area of activity, action taken on the basis of recorded written rules, and rules are implemented by neutral officials, career advancement depends on technical qualifications judged by organisation, not individual.
8. The Vohra Committee submitted its report in 1993. It maintains that the activities of crime syndicates/mafia organisations had developed links with and were being protected by government functionaries and political personalities, *The Times of India*, 13 May 2012.
9. *The Economic Times*, 11 January 2012
10. *Ibid.*
11. The UNDP Report 2010. Available at: *www.hdr.undp.org/en/reports/global/*hdr. Accessed on 201312/12/2011
12. The Department for International Development (DFID) Annual Report 2007.
13. *Ibid.*
14. The Indian Parliament adopted 86th Constitutional Amendment whereby elementary education has been made fundamental right in the Constitution.
15. Suresh R. Foreign Policy and Human Rights: An Indian Perspective, Madhav Books, Gurgaon, Haryana, 2009, p. 33.
16. The UNHCHR statement by Mary Robinson, United Nations High Commissioner for Human Rights World Summit on Sustainable Development Plenary Session Johannesburg, South Africa, 29 August 2002. Available at: *www.un.org/events/wssd/statements/unhchrE.htm.* Accessed on 12/12/2011.
17. The Extent and Nature of Absolute Poverty Final Report to DFID: R8382.
18. The Right to Information Act, 2005 empowers the people to seek information on any matter except some documents related to defence, external affairs, etc. Right to Public Service and Citizen Charter empowers the people to get certain services form the government offices in a time bound manner.
19. In the human rights-based development approach people are recognised as key actors in their own development, rather than passive recipients of commodities and services. The participation of people is both a means and a goal. The strategies of rights based-approach are empowering. Again under this approach both outcomes and processes are monitored and evaluated. All programmes under this approach focus on marginalised, disadvantaged and excluded groups. The development process is locally owned. The programmes aim to reduce disparity. Under this both top-down and bottom-up approaches are used in synergy. The situation analysis is used to identify immediate, underlying and basic causes of development problems.

12

Concerns for Women: The Vision for 21st Century

Ruchi Ramesh

The twenty-first century undoubtedly belongs to women, but in India, it was in the nineteenth century that the women's concerns first came to be viewed seriously and remained in the public gaze. Today, when we have entered the twenty-first century or more accurately when one-and-a half decade of this century has passed, the construction of gender identity and the way in which the question of gender is being debated indicate that most of the issues related to women are still unaddressed or are not being dealt in a manner they should be. The issues related to women should be the main focus in the present century, not only because half of the population under the sky is that of women but because women bear almost all responsibility for meeting basic needs of the family. According to United Nation's data, 1.2 billion people live in extreme poverty, the majority of them are women and girls, two-third of the world's illiterate are women, majority of the millions of school age children not in school are girls. Today, women comprise nearly 60 per cent of all people living with HIV/AIDS in sub-Saharan Africa, and HIV/AIDS is rapidly becoming a disease of women as 76 per cent of the young people (aged 15-24 years) living with HIV are female. Despite this alarming trend, women know less than men about how HIV is transmitted and how to prevent infection. What little they do know is often rendered useless by the discrimination and violence they face and their relative powerlessness to refuse sex or negotiate safe sex, especially in the context of marriage.

Around the world food crisis has a severe impact on women. Millions of people eat two or three times a day, but a significant percentage of women eat only once and now many women are denying themselves even that one meal to ensure that their children are fed. The rate at which girls and women die in comparison to men is high in low- and middle-income countries than in high-income countries. The report estimated the number of excess female deaths (missing girls and women) at every age and every country in 1990, 2000 and 2008. Globally, excess female mortality after birth and "missing" girls at birth account for an estimated 3.9 million women below the age of 60. About two-fifth of them are never born, one-fifth go missing in infancy and childhood and remaining two-fifth do so between the ages of 15 to 59.[1]

It is important to empower a woman to make a society more resilient. The 2000-UN Millennium Development Goals (MDGs) recognises the intrinsic instrumental value of gender equality. The United Nations Millennium Declaration contains a statement of values, principles and eight specific goals and related targets that constitute an international agenda for the twenty-first century. The women-related issues are widely recognised; Goal 3 is "to promote gender equality and empower women" and the other seven Millennium Development Goals are related and also considered as essential for development. The MDG summit adopted a global action plan and resolution calling for action to ensure gender parity in education, health, economic opportunities and decision making through mainstreaming in development policy making. The resolution and action plan reflect the belief of the international development community that gender equality and women's empowerment are development objectives. Gender equality is core concern and an essential part of human development. The extent of discrimination can be measured through the Gender Inequality Index (GII). The higher the GII value the greater the discrimination. Based on 2012 data for 148 countries, the GII shows large variations across countries, ranging from 0.045 (in Netherlands) to 0.747 (in Yemen), with an average of 0.463.

India ranks 132 with 0.610 GII in the world. The three key factors for the persistence of high gender disparities in India are low female representation in parliament (10.9 per cent), gender imbalance in educational achievement (26.6 per cent of women have completed at least secondary education, compared with 54.4 per cent of men) and low labour force participation (29.0 per cent of women are in the labour force, compared with 80.7 per cent of men).

Gendered Economics

The observation of Dr B.R. Ambedkar, the architect of the Indian Constitution seems highly relevant in today's context. While introducing the Indian Constitution in the Constituent Assembly, Dr Ambedkar observed: "On the 26th January, 1950 we are going to enter into a life of contradictions. In politics we will have equality and in social and economic life we will have inequality. In politics we will be recognising the principle of one man one vote and one vote one value. In our social and economic life, we shall by reason of our social and economic structure, continue to deny the principle of one man one value. How long shall we continue to live this life of contradictions? How long should we continue to deny equality in our social and economic life? If we continue it for long, we will do so only by putting our political democracy on peril. We must remove this contradiction at the earliest possible moment, or else those who suffer from inequality will blow up the structure of political democracy which this Assembly has laboriously built up."

The social and economic factors are closely interwoven to determine the position and condition of women in society. Many socio-cultural ethos are responsible for placing women low on economic front and vice-versa. The central objective of development is gender equality. This year's (2014) theme for International women day was 'Equality of Women is progress for all'. Across the world, women and men access economic opportunities fundamentally in different ways—in wage employment, agriculture or in entrepreneurship. The more involvement of women can enhance productivity, make the institution more representative and improve the outcomes for the next generation. Many researchers suggest that when a woman's economic status improves, so does that of her household, her community and, potentially, her country. Over half a billion women have joined the world's labour force over the last 30 years as women's participation in paid work has risen in most of the countries of the developing world. Everywhere women tend to earn less than their counterparts. It is contributed to the fact that women are more likely to work as unpaid family labourers or in the informal sector. Women entrepreneurs operate in smaller firms and less profitable sectors. According to World Development Report 2012, women now represent 40 per cent of the global force, 43 per cent of the world's agricultural labour force and more than half the world's university students. The agriculture sector is booming, yet food insecurity is at unprecedented levels. Global food production needs to double by 2050 to feed a projected population of 9 billion. In developing countries, women form the backbone of agriculture. They are responsible for 60 to 80 per cent of food production in most of the developing countries and half of the world food production. They serve as producers, labourers, processors and traders within largely domestic markets. They also dominate household-level food production and preparation.[2] For the last two decades, women have made their presence felt in professional and managerial ranks of many corporations at about the same rate as men, yet at senior level they remain dramatically underrepresented. As on June 2012, only 3.6 per cent of Fortune 500 CEOs are women, and women hold 15 per cent of Fortune 500 board seats and corporate executive positions. This situation is almost the same in most of other countries. In UK, women account for 4 per cent of CEOs and 15 per cent of board seats in the top 100 UK—headquartered companies; and in India, 11 per cent of large-company chief executives are women. Exception includes countries with a legal mandate for diversity like Norway where 40 per cent of board seats in public companies need to be held by women.[3] Individual positions are definitely influenced by stereotypes as long as more women are not in leadership positions the situation will continue to be "think-leader-think male" phenomenon and will remain a serious barrier to women's advancement.[4] Globalisation has also affected women and their lives to a great extent. It has reduced the ability of women to find the dignified and secure place for employment. The role of women has changed from traditional agricultural and domestic role to manufacturing and assembly production. The 12th Five Year Plan (2012-17) is aimed to improve employability of women, work participation rates, especially in organised sector, and increase ownership of assets and control over resources.

Women and Politics

Women's participation in political processes is not only important to strengthen the democracy but for their struggle against exclusion, marginalisation, trivialisation and oppression. India has a unique experience significantly different from other nations, as from the day one the Constitution framers wisely opted to give every citizen the right to vote, whereas country like America which pioneered republican democracy in 1787, women did not gain voting right till 1920. The Noble laureate Amartya Sen has rightly stated, "Democracy is not only the goal of development, it is primary means of development."[5] The effective bottom-up strategies adopted in India through Panchayati Raj campaign combine three factors: giving opportunity to the people at grassroots level to build self-reliance, key change agents empowering women and developing effective partnership with local government. Gandhiji had the vision of 'Self-ruling villages'. He was of the opinion that villages are to rule themselves in traditional manner through *sarpanch* and *panch* or there should be decentralisation of power and that centre government should have very limited power. On the contrary, Bhimrao Ambedkar's apprehension was that submitting the liberty and property to the hands of *panch* will perpetuate the traditional prejudices of the population. Dr Ambedkar's view was also endorsed by the World Bank research which explains that world over central governments tend to be more egalitarian than villages.[6] Recent constitutional mandate for political participation of women could hardly transcend institutionalised patriarchy. Entrenched ideologies assume that politics is world of men, and women's role is confined to the domestic domain. The 73rd and 74th Amendment Bills were presented in December 1992 and President gave his assent in April, 1993. The amendments were officially enacted through the issuance of government notifications the Constitution (73rd Amendment) Act, 1992 (commonly referred to as the Panchayati Raj Act) and went into effect on 24 April 1993, and the Constitution (74th Amendment) Act, 1992 (the Nagarpalika Act) on 1 June 1993 paving the way for the mandatory reservation of one-third of the positions for women in local bodies at all three levels. Constitution 110th and 112th Amendment Bills, 2009 increased reservation for women in PRIs (Panchayati Raj Institutions) and urban local bodies from one-third to half of the total number of seats. The Indian states which have already implemented 50 per cent reservation for women in PRIs are Bihar, Chhattisgarh, Madhya Pradesh, Kerala, Rajasthan, Uttrakhand and Himachal Pradesh. As on 25 November 2011, the states of Andhra Pradesh, Chhattisgarh, Jharkhand, Kerala, Maharashtra, Orissa, Rajasthan and Tripura also reserve 50 per cent of their posts for women. The Women Reservation bill which proposes a third of all seats reserved for women in Lok Sabha and state legislative assembly is yet to see the light of the day.

In India, giving power to women at the local level led to increase in the provisions of public goods, such as water and sanitation, which matter more to women The primary obstacles which make women weak planners and policy implementers in the local self-government, as delineated by women themselves, are burden of household work, lack of family and community support, lack of financial support, lack of political consciousness, cultural barriers and male domination in decision making. As the term of 15th Lok Sabha comes to an end the empowerment of women and increasing gender crimes and increasing concerns about women safety started resonating in our Parliament when remarks were made by congress vice-president Mr. Rahul Gandhi. Tribal women in Jharkhand urged Mr. Rahul Gandhi to give proper representation in Parliament and assembly election (February, 2014).

The Vice-President, Dr S Radhakrishnan stated that India must have a "socio-economic revolution...(to achieve) the real satisfaction of the fundamental needs of the common man...(and) a fundamental change in the structure of Indian society". Aristotle, the Greek philosopher, extensively wrote on the rights of citizens to property and participation in public affairs, but the concept of human rights suffered from various limitations, the slaves and maintain peace, as well as preserve and promote women rights with great expectation. In setting the world agenda for the twenty-first century it is important to understand the political, economic and social context within which change is taking place. George Orwell metaphorically illustrated in his Novel *Animal Farm* "All animals are equal but some are more equal than other", which goes well when we take in consideration the human rights of women. The Beijing Platform for Action and the Global Development Agenda from the MDGs to the Post-2015 Development Agenda, the 58th session of the Commission on Status of women has come out with the agreement that safety, human rights and empowerment of women as pivotal in the post-2015 debate (22 March 2014)[7] . The "CNN phenomenon" (Satellite communication) has revolutionised the women's rights. Various studies show that it is not that more rape cases or atrocities are taking place but it is that the slogan "speak up " has positive effect on women, more cases are being reported and very less or no cases go unnoticed. Even in America women are not safe. One out of every five woman is sexually harassed. According to a report of White House, more than 50 per cent of them were harassed before the age of 18 years. One out of every eight women's case comes to the notice of police. According to the report 33.5 per cent women were sexually harassed. 27 per cent women were of Indian or of Alaska origin, 15 per cent of Spanish, 22 per cent black and 19 per cent were white women. The study shows that in most of the cases men were known. In America than two crore and twenty thousand women and sixteen lakh men were sexually harassed[8] . Dr Ambedkar's view on women participation in light of the debate of Article 44 and uniform civil code under which all religion should have one laws related to women is worth mentioning here. He advocated unique laws for all women despite diverse religiosity. The first Prime Minister Jawaharlal Nehru stated that after ten years it will get implemented but till date it has not been implemented. Its implementation will undoubtedly pave the way for assertive women community.

Conclusion

The women do not constitute just one group among the various other groups in the society which are socially excluded, they are cross-cutting category of individuals that overlaps all other disadvantaged groups (poor, caste, class, religious minorities and so on). So, to empower women it not only needs institutional transformation but requires systemic transformation not just of any institutions, but changes in all structures which are specifically supporting patriarchy.[9] Many progressive recommendations were put forward by various governments, women organisations, civil societies and other international organisations for empowering women as economic, political and social actors. While domestic policy action is crucial, the international community can play a role in complementing these efforts in priority areas, and more generally, in supporting evidence-based public action through better data, impact evaluation and learning.

The economic empowerment of women is a contributing factor to achieve equality between women and men. But economically strengthening women—who are half the world's workforce—is not only a means by which to spur economic growth, but also a matter of advancing women's human rights. When governments, businesses and communities invest in women and when they work to eliminate inequalities developing countries are less likely to be plagued by poverty. Entire nations can also better their chance of becoming stronger players in the global marketplace. The gender sensitive policies, programmes, plans, schemes and action plans are documented by various international and national organisations, but the latest data is the testimony that their outcomes are not proportionate.

To be effective, these policies must target the root causes of gender gaps. In some areas, government needs to address binding constraints to progress as differential access to economic opportunities. Policies will be needed that tackle multiple constraints that come from the workings of markets and institutions to limit progress. In these cases, policy makers will need to prioritize these constraints and address them simultaneously and sequentially.

There are many obstacles to the realisation of social transformation through political change especially for the country which has not really reached that stage of political maturity for its women. Women still face many handicaps in the politics like resistance to devolving power and funds from centre (male) to periphery (female).[10] The legislative action has been reactive rather than proactive on women issues that give women greater representation in political office.[11] There is need to provide women with specific kind of support which will go beyond technical training. It is also necessary to strengthen women's sense of common identity by articulating the elements of feminist consciousness and presenting it as the special quality of women's leadership. The various feminist discourse and actions are essential to recommend the kind of leadership women will have. There is need for a more enabling environment to enable the women to act effectively in politics.

In spite of the widely held conviction of the elevated social status of women, the plight is only marginally changed. In order to break the barriers of entrenched customs and traditions, poverty and illiteracy women have to come out into the open to freely voice and participate in the political arena. They need to exert immense mental and physical strength. This strength can be achieved when economic status improves with education and awareness regarding problems and their solutions. Implementation of 73rd Amendment though at this point seems to have just about managed to increase participation of women in politics only numerically, without really contributing in changing governance qualitatively, its significance in long-term participation of women in mainstream politics and decision making cannot be ignored. An undeniable fact is that better access to knowledge of political institutions, training and capacity building of men and women alike can really contribute to human capital generation. The sensitisation and capacity building are some of the vital areas of intervention. Major government policies for overall development and capacity building of women more or less suffered due to lack of awareness on the part of women and also about the lack of sensitisation about various development programmes. The effective participation of women in politics should be achieved through training along with literacy educational programme. The special programmes on the role of women in PRIs, on rights of women and procedures should be prepared and disseminated through mass media.

In the first half of 2014 the general elections are due and the perceived change in the government is well debated and tackling of women issue is the challenge as well as opportunity for the new government. To catch up with the mainstreaming of women by end of the term (2019) should be high on the agenda of new constituted government. All possible efforts should be made by the government to give the long due share to women, so that India can emerge as just society. Closing the gender gap can enhance the economic productivity, improve development for next generation and make institutions and policies more representative.

Other than the efforts of the government change in culture is also required. The key element to change the culture should be men must learn to accept the rising power of women. They should also learn to share, care and live with half the nation which constitutes women.

NOTES AND REFERENCES

1. World Bank Report, 2012.
2. United Nations (2007), "Report of the Secretary-General: Strengthening Efforts to Eradicate Poverty and Hunger, Including Through the Global Partnership for Development (E/2007/71)", New York.
3. Global Agenda Council on Women's Empowerment 2011-2012.
4. Ibid.
5. Available at: http:/www.thp.org/india/panchayat.htm. Accessed on: [AQ: Please provide the date of accession.]
6. Swaminathan Aiyar (9 February 2014) Ambedkar vs Gandhi : The risks of village empowerment, *Times of India*, p. 9.
7. Available at: http://www.unwomen.org/en/news/stories/2014/3/executive-director-statement-on-csw58-outcome#sthash.d4huQyyh.dpuf. Accessed on: [AQ: Please provide the date of accession.]
8. Amar Ujala (25 January 2014), p. 16.
9. Narayan, Deepa (ed.) (2005), Measuring Empowerment, World Bank Washington DC.
10. Hazarika, Sujata D. (2008), Democracy and Leadership: The gendered Voice in Politics. *Sociological Bulletin, 61*(3) 353-370.
11. Mandira, Kala (2014), What Women Want, *India Today*, February, New Delhi.

13

Requirements for Road Safety in India

Piyush Tewari

From 31 August 1997 onwards, when the horrific death of Princess Diana in a road crash in France shocked the public and government in the United Kingdom, road safety received renewed attention in the European Union and across the world. Investigations into the crash found that the driver was impaired in his driving due to alcohol as well as the occupants of the car were not wearing seat belts. Following renewed public focus on Road Safety, the UK undertook a slew of measures including a seat belt and safety campaign and the EU reduced its Blood Alcohol Limit to 50 mg.

On 3 June 2014, in an almost eerie repetition of events, public discourse and outcry over the issue of Road Safety reached a helm in India when Union Cabinet Minister, Gopinath Munde died in a car accident in Delhi. On account of being seated in the rear of the vehicle, he was not wearing a seat belt either.

By 5 June 2014, in a matter of 2 days the Government at the center had announced that a stronger road safety law would replace the current Motor Vehicles Act, 1988—an archaic legislation which loosely covered Road Safety by regulating motorized transport in the country.

Will it always take a public death to bring about strong legislative change in Road Safety?

Background

Road traffic injuries are the eighth leading cause of death globally, and the leading cause of death for young people aged 15–29. More than a million people die each year on the world's roads, and the cost of dealing with the consequences of these road traffic crashes runs to billions of dollars.

A Comparative Data of Road Accidents in India over the last five years

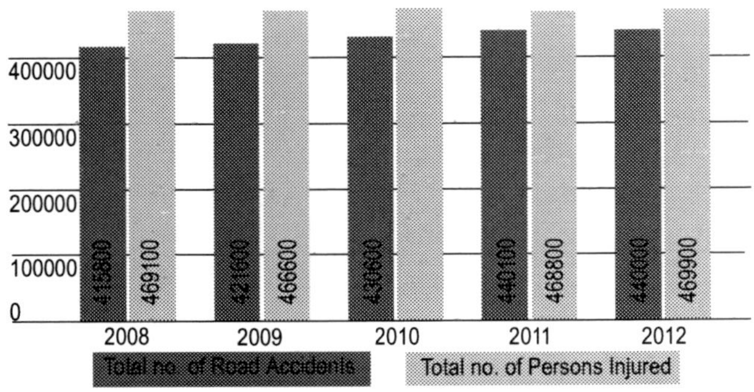

There has been a steady rise in the no. of deaths due to road accidents in the past 5 years

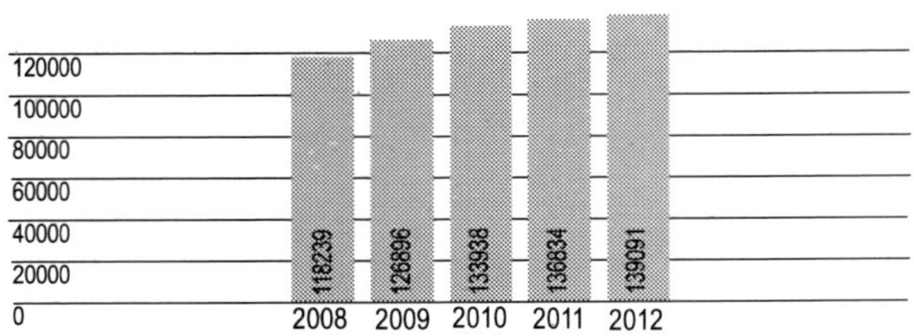

Source: National Crime Records Bureau, 2012.
www.savelifefoundation.org

According to the Global Status Report on Road Safety 2013, the overall global road traffic fatality rate is 18 per 100,000 population. However, middle-income countries have the highest annual road traffic fatality rates, at 20.1 per 100,000, while the rate in high-income countries is lowest, at 8.7 per 100,000.

Among the middle-income countries, India has one of the highest numbers of road accidents and the situation is only getting worse.

In the last 10 years, more than 1 million people have died in road crashes in India. The epidemic of Road Accidents affects the lives of more than 600,000 people annually, causing death, disability, and loss of livelihood, thereby pushing thousands of families into poverty and posing a massive burden on health care costs in the country. The Planning Commission estimates that the socio-economic cost of accidents is approximately 3 per cent of India's GDP. The highest risk factor is to vulnerable road users—close to 30 per cent of deaths are those of Vulnerable Road Users.

Road Traffic Injuries present a high burden of premature death in the country. The threat of death by a road accident is higher than those posed by HIV/AIDS, Diabetes and malaria. Yet, the number of interventions and amount of money spent on reducing road traffic injuries, is almost negligent. Road Accidents are also a leading cause of disability; they are among the top 10 contributors in India to Disability Adjusted Life Years (DALYs) or the number of years lost to a person due to living with a disability.

Legislative Legacy

The causes for India's exceptionally high number of crashes include bad road user behavior, flawed road design and engineering, weak enforcement of traffic laws and the lack of rapid trauma care. Legislatively, Road Safety and Traffic Management in India are weakly governed by the Motor Vehicles Act, 1988 and allied Central Motor Vehicles Rules, 1989 as well as the Rules of the Road Regulations 1989. However this combined body of rules and regulations lacks a basic principle—that of comprehensively addressing Road Safety in India. The Motor Vehicles Act, 1988 is a complex set of clauses governing licensing, vehicle standards and certain offences. But as the name itself glaringly points out, it is an Act that deals with motorized transport and omits to protect and regulate pedestrians, cyclists, cycle rickshaw drivers, children and old people, among others. These Vulnerable Road Users, who make up more than 50 per cent of road users in India are unregulated and unprotected legally and practically. Given India's rapid urbanization and motorization, the danger to vulnerable road users like pedestrians and cyclists is only going to increase. However, they currently have no protective barrier between them and motorized transport, either on the roads or in the statute books.

The Motor Vehicles Act was borrowed from its British counterpart in 1939 when a tumultuous India was just about getting used to roads and motorized transportation systems. In 1984, the Government realized that the 1939 Act needed significant updating—especially in the areas of licensing, regulation of new types of vehicles which were entering the market, more stringent punishment for certain offences and creating institutions for Road Safety Management in the form of Road Safety Councils—and started the process of redrafting the law. For 1988, it was a watershed Act; unfortunately the process of upgradation has remained stuck since then.

Motorized Transport and Road Safety

Despite being regulated, motorized transport poses a huge problem for road users as well. Regulations on motorized transport are archaic and have not kept up with the rapid motorization and urbanization that is taking place. The automobile industry in India produces nearly 4.6 million vehicles each year in addition to the 50 million already plying on the roads. 72 per cent of these vehicles are two wheelers.

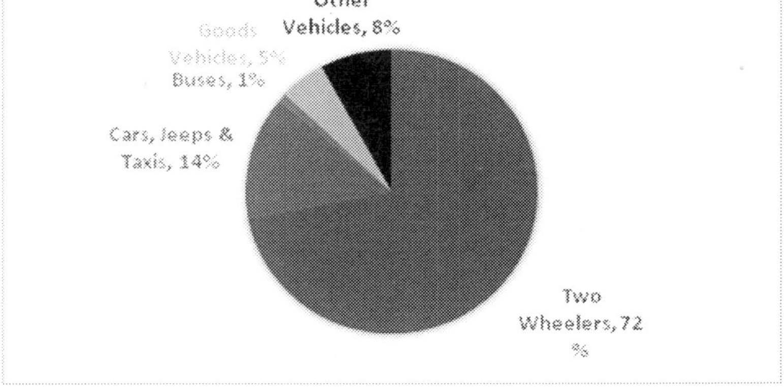

In India, most road accidents are blamed on the fault of the driver—more than 75 per cent of accidents are said to stem from "driver error". A vehicle in the hands of an untrained driver is akin to a weapon. Considering the number of accidents caused due to driver error, it can safely be said that almost 1.5 lakh additional murders happen with the vehicle as a weapon.

Despite these shocking facts, the two elements that control the quality of drivers on our roads—licensing and training—are either fractured or completely missing. The licensing regime in India is outdated and allows for excessive human intervention, leading to delays, corruption and lack of transparency in the system. In 2011-12 alone, Regional Transport Offices (RTO) across the country issued more than 1 crore, 18 lakh licenses. This scale coupled with the inherent inefficiencies of a manual system, results in lakhs of licenses being issued without prescribed checks and balances. Furthermore, studies show that thousands of drivers carry multiple licenses issued by different States unlinked to any central database. Mostly, licenses are granted for a period of 20 years without any intermediate checks to test the driving skills including health of the driver. Penalties for licensing offences continue to be low and rampant corruption makes it easy to escape crimes pertaining to licensing. Driver training in India is sparse and has not been made mandatory in the Motor Vehicles Act, 1988 for obtaining license. This is along with abysmal standards in respect to infrastructure and staffing of schools.

In order to wipe out issues related to licensing, the "Graduated Drivers' Licensing System (GDLS)" followed by many countries around the world is recommended. GDLS is designed to provide new drivers of motor vehicles with driving experience and skills gradually over time in **low-risk** environments. There are typically three steps or stages through which new drivers pass. They begin by acquiring a learner's permit, progress to a restricted, provisional or probationary license, followed by receipt of a full driver's license. GDLS also generally restricts nighttime, expressway, and unsupervised driving during initial stages, but lifts these restrictions with time and further testing of the individual, eventually concluding with the individual attaining a full driver's license.

Driver training, on the other hand, can be addressed by ensuring strict control over Driver Training Schools with a limited number of Government Training schools receiving approval every year by the law; a certification-of-passing of driver training, issued by an accredited driver training school, to be made mandatory for obtaining a driving license and tasking automobile manufacturing companies with establishing state-of-the-art driving schools in PPP mode with Central and State Governments. Foremost however, it is imperative that a driver training regimen be made mandatory in the law.

Non-motorized Transport and Road Safety

Global statistics shows that half of the world's road traffic deaths occur among motorcyclists (23%), pedestrians (22%) and cyclists (5%), i.e. "vulnerable road users". In India too, the statistics of road traffic deaths among VRU's is high with two-wheelers accounting for about 19.92 per cent (highest among all road users). Non-motorized transport in the country include Vulnerable Road Users like pedestrians, cyclists, children, senior citizens, passengers in auto rickshaws and those on two wheelers. Presently, there is no central legislation comprehensively governing their protection and regulation.

Source: National Crime Records Bureau, 2012. www.savelifefoundation.org

The right of way on the roads belongs equally, if not more, to non-motorized transport and Vulnerable Road Users. However, the roads are designed and engineered keeping in mind vehicles and the flow of traffic, not people. This often leads to increased accidents as roads designed for vehicles help in increasing speed, leading to an increase in road accidents.

Across the world, Vulnerable Road Users are regulated under specific statutes. In the United States, traffic safety is generally governed by state law which deals effectively with Motorists, cyclists, pedestrians; bicycle safety and Intersections & Traffic signals. For example, in California and Pennsylvania, a person riding a bicycle or operating a pedicab upon a highway has all the rights and is subject to all the provisions applicable to the driver of a vehicle. Hawaii defines vulnerable users as "pedestrians legally within a street" and roadway workers, as well as operators of bicycles, mopeds, wheelchairs, and other small vehicles. Hawaii's code, in an effort to deter aggressive driving, increases penalties for drivers who injure vulnerable road-users.

What India needs, to protect its Vulnerable Road Users, is a "Safe Systems Approach". The Safe Systems approach aims at creating a *forgiving* road system based on the fact that road users will make mistakes and they are vulnerable. Yes the system needs to be strong enough to mitigate the risk of mortality and morbidity. Safe System principles focus attention on the design and management of road infrastructure, vehicles and travel speeds: recognizing that road trauma levels are largely determined by the interaction of these key elements. The ultimate goal is to create an environment in which road users can withstand the physical forces generated in the event of a crash.

The Institutional Solution

Road Safety in India is a multi-agency issue with drivers' licensing and training falling under the ambit of RTO or transport department, road design and engineering falling under PWD to NHAI to Ministry of Urban Development, enforcement falling with the police and Home Ministry and emergency care coming under the ambit of the Health

Ministry. Any multi – agency issue requires a **lead agency** for its effective outcome or to achieve an estimated target. Internationally, it has been seen that developing countries that have invested in establishing a dedicated lead agency for road safety with a secretariat, budget and authority have had better outcomes in improving road safety than those who haven't. While India has a National Road Safety Council, there is no agency including the council that has a dedicated team, clear authority or sufficient budgets.

WHO and the World Bank's joint Report on Road Traffic Injury Prevention, 2004 identified the fundamental need for a lead agency in Government to guide the national road safety effort to facilitate evidenced-based decision making, control resources and coordinate efforts by all sectors of Government. Most countries who have managed to successfully reduce the number of road deaths have done so due to the presence of a strong, central, decision making agency. Argentina's **National Road Safety Agency** (ANSV), Sweden's Swedish Road Administration (SRA) who designed the renowned *Vision Zero* initiative in Sweden and the National Highway Traffic Administration (NHTA), a stand-alone lead agency in the United States are all successful examples of an agency taking the lead in managing road safety in the country.

A comprehensive Road Safety Law for India would be incomplete without a detailing of the structure, powers, functions and organization of a Lead Agency for the country.

Political Will

252 people died in terror attacks in 2012 in India. During any terror attack, India's Home Minister puts the nation on high alert after every attack while all major political parties release statements condemning the violence. In 2012, almost 1.4 lakh people died in road accidents in India while almost 5 lakh were critically injured or permanently disabled. Yet, there were no statements of outrage or sentiments condemning this abysmal state of Road Safety in the country. Terror attacks are unquestionably different in the fear and outrage that they inspire however in terms of loss of life, road crashes are a far more threatening menace.

While there has been a lackadaisical approach politically to address this problem, the recent demise of Mr. Gopinath Munde, a newly appointed Union Cabinet Secretary, seems to have awoken both the public and political class to this problem. The Government has been quick to effectively tackle the issue, by starting the process of drafting a new, comprehensive road safety law for the country. However, apart from passing a new law, the number of deaths will only increase with all parts of the system being addressed—including having new, stronger laws, enforcement that acts as a deterrent and seamless emergency care.

India is no stranger to eradicating a public health problem that has scale and magnitude. In 2011, India made unprecedented progress against the menace of polio, with the last official case being reported in the country. This was a battle that was waged since 1985, where over 200,000 cases of polio were reported nationally. It was only the Government's commitment, where it was ensured that the entire State apparatus was geared for the polio eradication programme down to the block and village level, that rid India of this epidemic. Road Accidents are another such public health epidemic that need to be dealt with an iron hand with the full backing of the political class and executive machinery.

The Role and Responsibilities of Traffic Police

Laws, rules, precautions or technology for road safety may amount to naught if the traffic police does not do its required policing / if traffic rules are not implanted. Many accidents could have been avoided if drivers followed traffic rules or traffic police ensure implantation of the rules. This is part of police reforms, which the Supreme Court has asked the states to implement. State police forces require a total make-over, so that they become professional and enjoy public's confidence. The new government must do the needful for ensuring a sea change for the police forces, not only for road safety, but also public and national security.

INDEX

A

Aam Admi Party (AAP), 72
Abdullah, Omar, J&K CM, 38, 42
Admiral D K Joshi, 57, 63
Admiral Sushil Kumar, Former Naval Chief, 57
Advanced Jet Trainers (AJT), 58
Advanced Light Helicopter (ALH), 59
Afghanistan, 53, 70, 77, 102, 103, 105, 111
Af-Pak region, 70
Africa, 85, 88, 98, 101, 109
African continent, 101
Air Defence Artillery, 61
Air Defence inventory and helicopter, 71
Air Power, 74
Aiyar, Mani Shankar, Indian Petroleum Minister, 91
AK-47, 37
Akhnoor, 40
Al-Qaeda, 33, 47, 103
Ambedkar, Dr. B.R., 161, 167, 169, 171
America's National Security Agency, 130
Amritsar, 40
Anantnag, 42
Andaman and Nicobar (A&N) Islands, 49
Andhra Pradesh, 170
Ansari, Hamid, Indian Vice President, 129
Antony, A K, the then Defence Minister of India, 39, 43, 55, 57
Argentina's National Road Safety Agency (ANSV), 182
Aristotle, the Greek philosopher, 170
Armed Forces Special Powers Act (AFSPA), 53, 152, 156
Army Aviation Corps (AAC), 60
Army Chief Gen Bikram Singh, 38, 53, 55
Army Chief Gen K Sundarji, 48
Army Day Parade, 53
ASEAN Summit, 2012, 95
ASEAN-China realtion, 97
Asia, 78, 110
Asian Balance of Power, 76-77
Asian countries, 92
Asian energy demand, 83
Asia-Pacific, 86
Assam, 34
ASSOCHAM, 50
Association of Police & Security Suppliers (APPSS), 49
Australia, 95, 98, 120
Awami League, 35

B

Backward Districts Initiative, 50
Balaganga, Shri N, 39
Bangladesh, 33-35, 70, 106, 108, 119
Barua, Paresh, 34
Bashir, Salman, Pakistani high commissioner, 43
Basic Trainer Aircraft (BTA), 58
Battalions, 76
Beijing Platform for Action, 171
Bharatiya Janata Party (BJP), 18-20, 24, 63-66, 127-28, 130, 133-34
Bhatkal, Yasin, Indian Mujahideen co-founder, 46
Bhutan, 104, 107, 133
Bhutto, Zulfikar, former PM of Pakistan, 33, 47
Bihar, 37, 170
Biotechnology, 123
Bofors gun, 59, 71
  scandal, 74
Boost employment, 73
Border Defence Cooperation Agreement (BDCA), 51-52

Brahmaputra (Yarlung Tsangpo) river, 52
Brahmos Hyper sonic missile systems, 111
Brazil, 83, 87, 119
BSF, 42
Buddhism, 95
Buddhist pilgrimage tourism, 78
Bullet-Proof Jackets (BPJs), 59
Bureau of Parliamentary Studies and Training (BPST), 29

C

Cameron, David, 20
Canada, 83, 110
Capt Ramesh Babu, 57
Central Asia, 98, 111
Central Motor Vehicles Rules, 1989, 177
Chakan Da Bagh, 40
Chennai, 50
Chenoy, Kamal Mitra, 21
Chetak and Cheetah helicopters, 61
Chhattisgarh, 63, 170
Chidambaram, P., India's former Home Minister, 76
China, 31, 35, 46, 47, 51, 52, 66, 69-72, 74-77, 79, 84-86, 88-91, 94-99, 107-09, 111, 119-22, 129, 134
  army, 32
  attack, 63, 93
  border, 134
  economy, 90, 121
  influence in Nepal, 107
  in Asia, 77
  intelligence, 34
  troops, 40
Chowdhury, Neerja, 21
Civilisation challenge, 70
Climate Change, 84-85, 102
CNN phenomenon, 171
Coalition government
  Compulsions of, 156
Coastal Security Scheme, 50
Cold war, 99
Commander Kuntal Wadhwa, 57
Committed bureaucracy, 154-55
Commonwealth, 111
Companies, 76
Confederation of Indian Industry (CII), 49
Congress party, 17
Congress-led UPA government, 128
Constitution (73rd Amendment) Act, 1992, 170
Constitution (74th Amendment) Act, 1992, 170
Constitution Amendment Acts, 153
Continuous and Comprehensive Evaluation (CCE), 144
Cross border terrorism, 65
Cross-border terrorism by Pakistan, 63
CRPF, 42, 76

D

Dafadar Inder Singh, 37
Defence industrial base, 73
Defence Manufacturers Association (DMA), 49
Defence Procurement Procedure (DPP), 50
Defence PSUs, 62
Defence Research and Development Organisation (DRDO), 66
Defence White Paper, 114
Delhi airport, 120
Department for International Development (DFID), 159
Developing housing structures, 117
Devyani Khobargade case, 110
Diana, Princess, horrific death of, 175
Diaspora Committee, 113
Disability Adjusted Life Years (DALYs), 177
Dravidian and Dalit communities, 66
DRDO, 62
Driver training, 179, 180

E

East Asia, 112
East Asian Crisis, 134
East China Seas, 99
Eastern Ladakh, 40
Economic Reconstruction, 73
Education System, 136
  Changing thought process, 139-40
  Gaps in, 137-39
  Purpose of, 136
  Reforms require, 146-50
    create more jobs, 149-50
    education programmes for parents, 147-48
    redesign government schools, 146-47
    redesign course curriculum, 148
    redesign examination system, 148

teachers' training, 147
System overhaul, 145
Why old system failing?, 141-45
Eid festival, 45
Emerging economies, 86
Empowerment training, 66
Energy security, 79, 80, 88, 91, 97
Energy, 20
Equality of Women is progress for all, 167
EU, 90
delegation, 113
Europe, 91
European Union, 175

F

Far East, 97
FDI, 66, 109
Fifth generation aircraft, 71, 74
Fifth generation fighter programme, 111
Finance, 20
Ford, 18
Foreign Correspondents Club of South Asia, 42
Fossil fuels, 87
Fourth Generation fighters, 71
France, 175
Fred W. Riggs, 154
Free Trade Agreements, 154

G

G-7
GDP, 90
OECD economies, 90
Gandhi, Indira, the then PM of India, 28, 33, 47, 48, 154
Gandhi, Rahul, 127, 128
Gandhi, Rajiv, former PM of India, 95, 155
Gandhi, Sonia, Congress President, 127-28
Gen Ashfaq Pervez Kayani, Pak army chief, 39
Gen V K Singh, former Army Chief, 59
Gender Inequality Index (GII), 170
Gendered Economics, 167
General Shankar Roychowdhury, 46
Germany, 120
Global energy, 82, 83
demand, 86
trade, 86
Global food production, 168
Global India, 159
Global oil supplies, 83
Global Status Report, 176
Gogoi, Tarun, Chief Minister, 35
Good Governance, 19, 21, 124, 134, 149, 151, 154-59, 162-63
Graduated Drivers' Licensing System (GDLS), 179
Great power, 62
Gujarat, 17, 18, 20, 21, 128, 130-32, 134
model, 132
Gulf Cooperation Council (GCC), 84
Gulf, 84, 98
population, 152
region, 152

H

Himachal Pradesh, 170
Himalayan kingdom, 107
Himalayas, 75
Hinduja, Srichand, Hinduja Group Chairman, 18
Hindutva government, 105
Hiranagar, 36, 37, 40
HIV/AIDS, 102, 165, 177
Human rights organisations, 72
human rights, 66
Hydrocarbon resources, 88
Hydrocarbon Vision 2025, 80
hydropower, 82

I

IB, 38
Ibrahim, Dawood, 33
India Air Force (IAF), 58, 71
India and Economic Inequality, 157-59
India and Myanmar
Bilateral relations between, 55
India and Social Inequality, 159-61
India and Sri Lanka
Relations between, 130
India is to achieve a global power, 18
India, 35, 37, 40, 41, 70, 71, 73, 75, 77, 79, 84-86, 89-91, 93-116, 118-24, 126-34, 151-62, 167, 169, 170,
bureaucracy in, 154
caste system, 160
construction industry, 122
democratic system, 24
developing, 159

economic development of, 19
energy mix, 81
national security, 73
nuclear power, 82
Parliament, 25
attack on, 33
disruption of, 26
powers of, 25
road safety in, 175-83
tank fleet, 71
India-ASEAN bilateral trade, 95
India-China
Border Areas, 52
GDP, 90
relation, 96, 97
Indian Army, 51, 74
Indian Coast Guard, 48
Indian Criminal Code, 159
Indian democracy, 100
Indian Diaspora, 98, 111-13
Indian economy, 73
Indian foreign policy
Challenges of, 93-104
Indian High Commission in Islamabad, 107
Indian Insurgent Groups (IIGs), 55
Indian National Congress, 23, 127
Indian Penal Code, 159
Indian silk and toy industry, 109
India-Pakistan war, 32
India-US dialogue, 36
Indonesia, 77, 97, 119
Indo-Pak war, 33, 67
Indo-Tibetan Border Police, 51
Infrastructure, 75
INS Vikramaditya, 97
Integrated Energy Policy, 81
Inter Services Intelligence (ISI), 33-34, 40, 47
Intermediate Jet Trainers (IJT), 58
Internal security sphere, 70
International Boundary, 33, 36, 37, 40, 47
International Energy Forum (IEF), 89
International Monetary Fund, 162
Iran, 83, 84, 91, 98, 106
Iraq, 77, 83, 84, 91
ISIS, Militant group, 134
Israel, 77, 106
Israel Military Industries, 59
IT services, 123
IT superpower, 157
Italy, 129, 131

J

Jai Jawan, 64
Jammu and Kashmir (J&K), 33, 36
Pak-sponsored terrorism in, 42
terrorist violence in, 70
Jantar Mantar, 7
Japan, 20, 76-78, 80, 84, 86, 89, 90, 91, 96, 97, 112, 113
Japan-China relation, 97
Jawaharlal Nehru University, 21
Jharkhand, 170
Jihadi terrorists, 72
Jihadi, 75
JPC, 27

K

Kalu Chak, 36
Karachi, 34, 47
Kargil Review Committee, 74
Kargil war, 49, 133
Kargil, 47
Karkare, Mr Hemant, 49
Karzai, Hamid, Afghanistan President, 133
Kashmir Valley, 41, 45, 46
Kathua, 37, 40
Kautilaya's *Mandala*, 105
Kautilya, 103-04
Kerala, 170
Khurshid, Salman, External Affairs Minister, 38, 44, 46
Koirala, Sushil, Nepal's Prime Minister, 133
Kolkata, 54, 56, 108, 116
Korea, 90, 112
Kothari Commission, 140
KPMG, 50
Kupwara, 42
Kuwait, 98, 112

L

L.M. Singhvi Committee Report, 113
Lahore, 34, 47
Lakshadweep and Minicoy (L&M), 49
Land for Peace, 33
Lashkar-e-Taiyyaba (LeT), 33, 40, 47
Late Shri K Raghuramayya, 28
Latin America, 85, 98, 101
LCA, 74

Leadership training, 66
Li Keqiang, 51
Libya, 84
Line of Actual Control (LAC), 40
Line of Actual Control, 33
Line of Control (LoC), 33, 37, 39, 40, 41, 43
Line of Control, 44
Look East Policy, 95
Lt Col Bikramjit Singh, 37
Lt Gen (retd.) Prakash Katoch, 51
Lt Gen Dalbir Singh, Eastern Army Commander, 54
Lt Gen Raj Kadyan, 45
Lt Gen S K Sinha, 30, 35
Lt Gen Vijay Oberoi, 60

M

Madhya Pradesh, 8, 170
Mahajan, Smt Sumitra, speaker of Lok Sabha, 29
Maharashtra, 48, 170
Maharashtra's coastline, 49
Mahatma Gandhi National Rural Employment Guarantee Programme (MGNREGP), 134, 153
Malaysia, 77
Maldives, 70, 106, 108
Malhotra, Rajiv, 66
Malik, Muhammad Yasin, 46
Manipur, 34
Maoist insurgency, 75
Maoists, 75
Maritime security, 99
Mass-transport systems, 117
Maxwell, Neville, Australian journalist, 63
Medium artillery guns, 74
Medium Guns, 71
Medium Multi-Role Combat Aircraft, 61
Metro rail network, 118
MiG fighters, 61
MiG-21, 71
Military Modernisation, 70, 74
Millennium Development Goals (MDGs), 166
Modi Means Business, 20
Modi, Narendra Damodardas, PM of India, 17-21, 23-24, 67, 70, 94-99, 109-10, 112-14, 127-33
    government, 19, 102-04, 109, 111, 134
    Wave, 17
Modi's speeches at election meetings, 19
Most Favoured Nation (MFN), 41, 106
Motor Vehicles Act, 1988, 175, 177-79
Mukherjee, Pranab, President of India, 55
Mumbai (26/11), 50
    bombings in, 33
    terror attacks, 49, 59, 106
Munde, Gopinath, Union Cabinet Minister, 175, 183
Muridke, 34, 47
Myanmar Naga Hills (MNH), 56
Myanmar, 35, 54-56, 95, 98-100, 106

N

Naga insurgent group, 56
Nagaland, 34
Naidu, Shri Venkayya, 29
Narasimha Rao government, 95
Naresh Chandra Committee, 74
Nathu La, 32, 47, 48, 67, 96
National Crime Records Bureau, 180
National Democratic Front of Bodoland (NDFB), 56
National Highway Traffic Administration (NHTA), 182
National Level Meeting (NLM), 56
National Maritime Authority, 65
National Road Safety Council, 182
National Security Adviser (NSA), 61-62
National Security Agenda, 70
National Security, 7, 72
NATO forces, 102
Naval Build-up, 74
Naval sphere, 71
Naxal-Maoists, 34, 35
NCC training, 64
NDA government, 110
NDA-1 regime, 96, 99, 104
Nehru, Jawaharlal, former PM of India, 26, 93, 127, 171
    dynasty, 13
Nepal, 70, 98, 106, 107
Netherlands, 170
New Cold War, 88
New Delhi, 40, 70, 72, 74
New Generation Smarter
    What Makes?, 136-37

New Great Game, 88
New Scramble for Africa, 88
New Zealand, 120
NGOs, 72
Nixon, Richard, late US President, 132
Non Aligned Movement (NAM), 93
non-OECD countries, 85
non-OPEC output, 87
North East, 34
North Korea, 152
North Waziristan, 46
Norway, 168
Nuclear
  deterrence, 75
  energy, 86

O

Obama, Barack, US President, 20, 36, 131
Operation Green Hunt, 72, 76
Orange Revolution or Arab Spring, 72
Ordnance Factories, 62
Orissa, 170
Orwell, George, 171

P

PAC, 27, 28
Pak army's BAT, 43
Pak's military-mullah combo, 42
Pakistan Occupied Kashmir (PoK), 45
Pakistan, 31-34, 36, 38, 40, 44, 46-47, 71, 72, 75, 76, 94, 95, 103, 105-06, 108, 119, 128-30, 133
Pakistan's Army, 33
Pakistani jihadi, 40-41
Pakistani Taliban, 103
Panchayati Raj, 169
Parikh, Mr. Kirit, 81
Paris based International Energy Agency, 98
Patahankot-Jammu National Highway (NH 1A), 37
People Welfare Programme, 155
People's Liberation Army (PLA), 48, 56
People's Revolutionary Party of Kangleipak (PREPAK), 56
PGLA Platoons, 76
Philippines, 77
PLAAF, 71
Pokhran II, 94, 133
Police Modernisation Scheme, 50
Poorest India, 159
Port Blair, 50
post-9/11 world system, 96
Powell, Nancy, US Ambassador, 110
President Xi Jinping, 129
PRIs (Panchayati Raj Institutions), 170
  role of women in, 174
PSUs, 62
Pulwama, 42
Punjab, 40

Q

Qatar, 84

R

Radhakrishnan, Dr S, 170
Rajasthan, 170
Ranade, Mr Jayadeva, 51
Rao, M S, 37
Rapid economic growth, 117
Rashtriya Swayamsevak Sangh (RSS), 21, 104, 134
Red Corridor, 35
Regional Operating Centres (ROC), 49
Regional Transport Offices (RTO), 179
Remote Operating Stations (ROS), 49
Republic of Korea, 91
Research and Analysis Wing (RAW), 39
Right to Information (RTI) Act of 2005, 152, 162, 164
Road Safety 2013, 176
Road Safety Councils, 178
Road Safety Management, 178
Road Traffic Injuries, 176-77
Robinson, Mary, 161
Russia, 77, 96, 97, 110, 111
Russia-Japan relations, 97
Russian Bear/Backfire, 75

S

SAARC countries, 104, 133
Saeed, Hafiz, 38
Safe Systems Approach, 181
Samba, 36, 37, 40
Saudi Arabia, 84, 87, 98, 106, 151
Science and technology, 99
Second World War, 100
Sectoral Level Meeting (SLM), 56
Security Forces operations, 72
Self-ruling villages, 169
Shanghai Cooperation Organisation (SCO), 114

Sharif, Nawaz, Pakistani PM, 38, 44, 130
Sharma, Shashi Kant, Defence Secretary, 58
Shaun Hipgrave, 49
Shinzo Abe, Japanese Prime Minister, 132
Short Service Commission, 65
Sikkim, 32, 47
Simla talks, 47
Singapore, 120
Singh, Dr. Manmohan, Former PM of India, 36, 51, 95, 128, 160
Singh, Dr Swaran , 52
Sino-Indian border problem, 96
Sino-Japan relationship, 77
Sir Creek, 107
Sopore, 42
South Africa, Whites in, 161
South Asia, 42, 106, 109
South China Seas, 99
South Korea, 77, 89, 97, 120
Southeast Asia, 95, 109
Sowars Kiran Kumar, 37
Sri Lanka, 106-08, 130
Standard Exchange Procedures (SEP), 107
Stealth fighter development, 111
Strategic Policy paper, 114
Strength, Weakness, Opportunities and Threats (SWOT), 105
SU-30 Fighters, 74
Supreme Court, 35
Sweden's Swedish Road Administration (SRA), 182
Switzerland, 107
Syed Ali Shah Geelani, 45
Syria, 106

T

Taj Mahal Hotel, 40
Tamil-dominated areas, 108
Tata Motors, 18
Thailand, 120
The Asian Age, 38
The Tribune, 60
Think-leader-think male, 168
Third world unity, 101
Thorn in the throne, 111
Tibet, 96
Tourism, 73
Tripura, 170
Tunda, Abdul Karim, 46
Turkey, 89

U

UAE, 84, 98
Ukraine crisis, 110
UNDP Report, 158
United Kingdom (UK), 49, 168, 175
United Liberation Front of Asom (ULFA), 34-35, 56
United National Liberation Front (UNLF), 56
United Nations (UN), 38-39, 102, 158-60
  treaty, 160
United States (US), 33, 77, 79, 83, 90, 91, 93, 96, 105, 110-11, 113, 130-31, 181-82
  drawdown from Afghanistan, 70, 105
  economy, 90
  trade center, terrorist attack on, 94
Universal values, 161
Unpleasant incidents, 54
UPA, 7, 8, 12
  administration, 72
  government, 10, 70, 76, 106
  Legacy of, 9
Urban
  areas, 119
  planners, 118
  population, 116
Urbanisation, 116
US Congressional Research Service (CRS), 18
US-China, 97
USSR, 93
  collapse of, 93
Uttrakhand, 170

V

Vajpayee, Atal Behari, former PM of India, 96, 104, 133
Vajpayee-Putin meet, 97
Verma, Bharat, Editor, Indian Defence Review, 58
Vietnam, 97
Vinayak Damodar Savarkar, 104
Violation of rights, 162
Vision Zero, 182
Vohra Committee Report, 1993, 155
Vulnerable Road Users (VRU), 180-81

W

Wagah, 40
Wang Yi, Chinese Foreign Minister, 129-30
War Memorial, 65
Washington DC, 36
Weapons System Integrated (WSI), 59
Weber, Max, 154
West Asia North Africa (WANA), 84
West Asia, 105, 106, 111
Western world, 98, 100
What-China-will-think, 111
White House, 171
WHO, 182
World Bank, 115, 122, 162, 169, 182
World Development Report 2012, 168
World food crisis, 166
World Trade Organisation, 162
World War I, 32
World War II, 32

Y

Yameen, Abdulla, Maldivian President, 108
Yemen, 166

Z

Zackaria, Fareed, 20